MEDITATIONS

BY DEREK JAMES MORRILL

CHAPTER HEADINGS • *Meditations*

MEDITATIONS

BY DEREK JAMES MORRILL

A Davidson-Hall Publication
Byworth, Petworth
West Sussex GU28 0JL

© 1996 Jean Morrill

ISBN 0 9529403 1 0

All rights reserved. No part of this work may be reproduced or stored in an information retrieval system (other than for the purposes of review) without the express premission of the Publisher or the Author in writing.

Design & Typeset by Catherine House Design in Jansen Monotype
Printed and bound by D. Isom (Printer) Ltd. of Herne Bay.

REVD. DEREK JAMES MORRILL was born on 23rd January 1930 in Eltham. He was educated at Eltham College and Southampton University, where he was awarded a First Class Honours Degree in Mathematics and Chemistry and a Ph.d in Organic Chemistry. He worked for the Chemical Company, I.C.I.. both in India and the UK for a total of twentynine years, until 1983.

In 1980 he started training for the Ministry, studyig at Northern College, Manchester and at Westminster College, Cambridge. On completion of his training, he accepted the invitation to serve the Churches of th West Sussex Area Ministry, and settled in Petworth with his wife, Jean. He was inducted at his Ordination Service on 18th June, 1983 at the Billingshurst Church.

A computer literate Minister with a great love of music, Derek Morrill loved to play the piano and the organ. He was a skilled carpenter and handyman and he carried out major restoration to the organ in the Manchester Church where he worshipped, saving the Church a significant repair bill. In Petworth he helped install the central heating system in the lower rooms of the Church.

He was connected with the Scouting Movement frm the age of seven. At the age of sixteen he became a Scout Leader, and eventually served as Assistant District Commissioner.

He enjoyed gardening and had looked forward to his retirement, when he planned to improve the garden of his home. The year before he was due to retire he died, after several months of ill-health and major surgery.

Always interested in history and archaeology, Derek Morrill used his wide knowledge to put many of the Biblical stories into an historic context in his sermons and meditations.

The *Meditations* were written during Derek Morrill's Ministry in the United Reformed Church, where he served the Churches of the West Sussex Area Ministry (Petworth, Billingshurst and Pulborough) from 1983 until his death in 1993.

Jean Morrill has arranged for the publication of this book and it is her wish that all sales profits should go to **The Children's Liver Disease Foundation.**

CHAPTER ONE

Preparing the Way 7

CHAPTER TWO

God Incarnate 25

CHAPTER THREE

Christ's Life and Work 41

CHAPTER FOUR

The Early Chruch 103

CHAPTER FIVE

God with Us 127

CHAPTER ONE

Preparing the Way

The Spirit of Knowledge and Fear of the Lord

O LORD our God, we come to You today as Your people,
believing in the arrogance of our small minds that we know You,
that we understand You;
Wanting to be Your servants, doing Your will in the world,
and believing most of the time that we know just what that will is.
And then Your Word brings us up short.
For in it we catch a glimpse of a vision of Your greatness,
and we remember what we have indeed been told from the beginning
and we are ashamed.
For we know, in that moment of vision,
that we have been far from realising how great You are,
or how small is our understanding and knowledge of Your majesty and glory.
Yet, Lord, small and insignificant as we are,
we know that You are never far from us.
We know too how much You want us to understand You,
to know You; to love and serve You,
for we have seen You too in the gift of Your Son, Jesus,
and heard His call to follow,
and we would obey that word.
Cleanse us form our arrogance, Lord.
Visit us with the gifts of Your Holy Spirit.
Grant us to know You more truly and to be patient in listening for Your Word,
to wait upon You and renew our strength for Your service;
a service not based upon our individual understanding,
nor upon the understanding of our human groupings,
but that service which can only be given by a mighty army
all under a single command.
The host of heaven were completed at Your call
and not one is missing from their number.
So, Lord, call together the host of earth,

that our number too may be complete, and all may know the greatness of our God.
Lord, in Your mercy,
Hear our prayer.

Eden and the River of Life

BILLINGSHURST 3RD NOVEMBER 1991
PETWORTH WOMENS OWN, 27TH FEBRUARY 1992

WHERE will we find Eden today?
And what will we find there?
The ancient writings speak of the garden of God.
They raise a vision, a dream, before our eyes.
A vision of a place of innocence and beauty,
whose trees and flowers surpass all those of earth.
A place where God Himself walked in the cool of evening
and spoke with His people,
people created and appointed to tend the garden.
It was a place of life,
and in it grows the tree of life,
God's own tree from which all life comes.
Watered by the mighty river,
the source of the rivers which girdle the earth,
carrying life to every part and every being.
A place of peace and repose,
of happiness and contentment,
a place where man and woman could dwell at peace with God
in Paradise.

But where is it today?
Even as we ask the question,
the vision fades.
It was in the mystic East,
somewhere far off, before the sunrise,
and it has receded behind a barrier of deep darkness.
For man,
who has never known the true glory of the love of God,

CHAPTER ONE • *Preparing the Way*

is impatient for Paradise;
is not content to wait and accept the gifts which God can bestow,
but would seek to wrest them from Him before their time!
Who demands of God as an equal
those things which God would give as a Father,
to the child He loves.
And the power of darkness dwells in that demand.
Seeking through it to gain entrance to Eden itself,
which cannot be.
And so,
as we,
today's representatives of mankind,
pursue our quest,
nothing is seen in the East,
save only the guardian angel
with his flaming sword of justice,
convicting us by his presence of our guilt and sin,
denying passage to us who would enter therein
bearing our load of that darkness which would deny God's light.

But God was not content to be alone
as He walked through the peace of paradise.
For Paradise without the companionship of love
is incomplete.
He would not abandon to the darkness
those parts of His creation whom darkness had overcome,
and wrested from Him.
Neither would He let the vision fade entirely into the gloom.
There are always dreams,
dreams of what might have been,
but cannot be.
A new way had to be opened,
so that that which might have been,

might be again.
The darkness must be overcome,
and banished from this road,
that though the battle might be fought again,
darkness and light confronting one another
through countless ages,
the issue should not be in doubt.
The light of God's Word came into the world
seeking out the darkness,
destroying it at its point of action,
in the lives of men and women,
by the power of His love.
Then was a new vision granted,
and a new way opened,
that paradise, once lost, might be regained.
The way to the East was closed
by God's eternal word.
Mankind could not tread that road again.
On the road to the West there lay a sunset barrier
guarded by the darkness of death.
But when that barrier was breached
and the road lay open,
the vision was renewed.
Beyond the sunset we see again
the place where God dwells,
the Holy City where God walks with His people in the cool of evening.
And there is no darkness there
for His light has banished the darkness.
And we see a garden there,
watered by the river which flows from His throne.
By that river stands the tree of life,
giving of its substance to all who would drink of the waters.
for now the fruit is ripe,

CHAPTER ONE • *Preparing the Way*

and the tree has healing in its leaves for all who ask.
All this is the victor's heritage,
God's loving gift to those in whom the darkness has been overcome.
The power which guile could not steal
is given instead in love.
The deep need which disobedience can not satisfy
is met in full by loving acceptance.

Lord, when today we seek the vision of Eden,
turn our eyes away from the past,
guide our thoughts away from what might have been,
to look instead at that which truly is.
To look beyond the sunset at the brightness of that light
which streams from Your realms into the whole of creation,
forever contending with the dark,
and beating it eternally,
that day and night might truly be alike in Your presence.
Help us to live always in that light,
and banish from our lives all the darkness of sin,
all the gloom of fear and despair,
that we may walk with confidence that westward road,
beyond the sunset,
to Eden.
Amen.

Psalm 23

SIX short verses of Scripture,
a source of strength and comfort for perhaps 3000 years.
Words which have gained in meaning from the coming of Jesus,
but which are themselves timeless,
and infinitely valuable.
'The Lord is my shepherd; I shall not want.
He maketh me to lie down in green pastures:
He leadeth me beside the still waters.
He restoreth my soul:
He leadeth me in the paths of righteousness for His name's sake.
Yea, though I walk through the valley of the shadow of death,
I will fear no evil;
for Thou are with me;
Thy rod and Thy staff, they comfort me.
Thou preparest a table before me in the presence of mine enemies:
Thou anointest my head with oil;
my cup runneth over.
Surely goodness and mercy shall follow me all the days of my life:
And I will dwell in the house of the Lord for ever'.

These are surely words which have arisen from a great depth of experience,
from one who knows that life has light and darkness;
that the souls of men can suffer great weariness and torment.
They come from one who has known the valley of the shadow,
the darkness which cannot be avoided,
the danger which must be faced.
And yet there is a deeper experience,
There is a source of steadfast love which is always available,
a supply which is never exhausted,
and it is there come rain or sunshine,

CHAPTER ONE • *Preparing the Way*

always faithful, eternally true to its own nature,
that nature which is love itself.

Our shepherd will guide our feet.
He will not fail to meet our deepest needs
nor leave us in the time of that need.
Even in a time of trouble He will lead us into places of peace,
places where we can share our delights with one another,
and with Him.
He calls us to eat and drink,
and to renew our strength,
and He Himself provides the bread of the green pasture,
the wine of those still waters
and bids us eat and drink that our souls may be restored;
that we may be filled with His peace.
Yet so often when we come to interludes of peace,
to visions of the beauty of His creation,
we forget from whence these things come.
When life is difficult
and yet suddenly there comes an assurance.
Things will work out alright.
There will be time enough for the tasks in hand,
and all will be well,
So often we do not acknowledge the source of that sudden strength
or of that vision of purpose and order.
Yet our shepherd is still with us.
Even though we forget,
He watches over us still
and His steadfast love never fails.

There is a voice which speaks to us as we go along life's road,
a voice which says 'Not that way, but this'.
'This is the best path'

CHAPTER ONE • *Preparing the Way*

Yet we do not always hear,
and sometimes we will not listen.
Sometimes we may wonder with suspicion,
why the voice is speaking in that way.
But our shepherd will not turn away,
will not, like us, give up in disgust,
for He speaks for the sake of His good name,
that name of steadfast love which never fails.

He has walked the pathways of life with our fathers' fathers,
and with many generations before that.
And he walks all the darkest pathways at our side.
Even that darkest pathway of all He has trod before us.
He knows every twist and turn of death's dark valley,
And in His care we shall find the sunrise beyond those gloomy walls
with a table laid before us which is filled with good things
A place where the powers of evil may not come.
Yet, in His name we may come there
and share in the food which He offers.
And will we not find on that day that we have seen that table before
in other, paler, guise?
Shrouded in the mists of this world.
And that we have tasted of its joys
in bread and wine,
amid those green pastures and still waters we have enjoyed?

It shall be so
For His goodness and mercy are eternal.
Our shepherd was before time began
and will be after it has ended.
His mansions were built before the stars were placed in the skies,
and they will endure for ever.
And he calls us into His fold,

CHAPTER ONE • *Preparing the Way*

and seeks for us when we are lost.
He rescues us from the power of our enemies,
and gives His life that we might live in Him.

Lord, help us to hear Your voice,
teach us to know You truly,
and grant us the grace to know that we are for ever members of Your flock.
We ask it in the name of the Shepherd,
the name of Jesus Christ, our Lord and Saviour. Amen.

CHAPTER ONE • *Preparing the Way*

Jethro and his Work

HAVE you ever thought about how Moses came to know about God. Of course we all know about him meeting with God at the burning bush on Mount Horeb, the sacred mountain, but he must have known about Him before that or he could not have begun to understand what was happening on that day. Yet we know that he had been brought up as an Egyptian, and he looked and spoke like an Egyptian. The shepherd girls who first met him in Midian called him an Egyptian when they spoke to their father about him. There was no way in which he would have learned about the God of the Israelites in an Egyptian palace. His mother cared for him in infancy, we are told, but then delivered him to the princess of Egypt.

Yet Moses became the outstanding religious leader of his people, only overshadowed by the Son of God Himself. The only place in his recorded history where he could have acquired the basic knowledge necessary to underpin his later understanding and personal knowledge was in Midian, in the period he spent in the household and family of Jethro, or Reuel, as he is also called, and Jethro was the priest of Midian and presumably the repository of all the religious knowledge of the tribe. And so he must have been the man through whom God chose to make Himself known to one of the greatest of His servants, the man on whom in great measure the whole of our faith and understanding rests.

We know little about him, for there are only a few references in the Bible and we have to read between the lines a bit to try to understand him. But perhaps we could get a little better picture through the eyes of one of his daughters. We don't know her name, only one of the seven daughters is named in the Bible, but perhaps that doesn't matter too much for his imaginative excursion into history.

I remember Moses all right.
I ought to, he married my sister Zipporah.
I remember the day he first came to us.
It was a great blessing to us that day.
We are a nomadic people,
we live by our herds of sheep and goats,
And I and my sisters have all looked after our flocks
ever since we were old enough to do so.
It had been a hot day and we had walked far with the flock
In the evening we came to the well and drew water.

CHAPTER ONE • *Preparing the Way*

But then the other shepherds came,
and we had to draw water for them to use
before we were allowed to use any ourselves.
It often happened and there wasn't anything we could do about it.
But this evening there was a stranger at the well.
He was an Egyptian by his dress, and by his speech.
He was tall and strong,
the sort of man who can look after himself in a fight.
He objected to what the other shepherds were doing, and told them so.
And they backed down.
None of them wanted to pick a fight with him.
And he helped us water the flock.
Afterwards he came home with us,
and our father welcomed him into our tents.
They liked one another from the start,
and since Moses was looking for somewhere to live
he came and joined our family.
He lived with us for a long time, many years.
And it wasn't long before he became truly part of the family,
for, as I said, he married Zipporah.
We thought he would be with us for ever,
but it didn't work out quite like that.

We soon found out that he wasn't an Egyptian at all
although he had been brought up as one.
Brought up in the royal palace in fact.
But he had found out that he was really an Israelite,
and he had been trying to find out more about his own people.
They were all living as slaves in Egypt,
but he had had to run away to save his life.
And now he needed to talk to someone who could explain the traditions of his people.
Our father knew these traditions, because we shared them.
He was the priest to our tribe, a man who knew God,

CHAPTER ONE • *Preparing the Way*

And in a way we were related,
for we could trace our ancestry back to Abraham.
The mother of our tribe was Keturah,
the wife of Abraham's old age.
His inheritance passed to Isaac, his son,
but we shared in his wisdom
and in his knoweldge of God.
So Jethro and Moses spent much time talking of these things,
and he thought very deeply about them all.
One thing about being a shepherd, you do get time to think about things
And then, one day we were camped near Horeb.
Moses took his part of the flock onto the lower slopes of the mountain
and he had a vision there.
God came and spoke to him personally and gave him a job to do.
A tremendous job.
To rescue his people from Egypt.
We had all heard about the power of the Pharoah
and of the strength of his armies.
It sounded almost impossible.
Moses wasn't very happy about it.
'How can I do this thing?' he asked when he came home.
'But I cannot deny the living God'.
And he and Aaron went off
They took Zipporah and the child with them at first,
but later they sent them back to live with us.
They thought that Egypt would be too dangerous for them.
I don't know what went on there, but there were away for many months.
I believe it was quite exciting.
When they came back there were thousands of people with them,
All the Israelite people rescued from slavery.
Some were wounded, they had fought a battle on the way
They did not mix much with our people
and they could not stay around for long.

CHAPTER ONE • *Preparing the Way*

There wasn't enough pasture for the animals.
In our sort of country you have to move on to where the grass is,
or all the animals will die.
But I know that Moses was recognised as the leader,
and as a prophet.
He had changed since that meeting with God.
Before he was interested in religion,
but now it was something more than interest.
He knew God for Himself.
And there was a kind of power about him,
Something you couldn't help noticing whenever he came near.
He had always been a strong man,
One who had that air of authority.
I suppose it came from his upbringing.
But this was something different,
It wasn't just worldly authority,
it was something stronger, greater than that.
Something to do with God Himself I think.
He was still learning how to use this power and authority.
At first he tried to do everything himself,
Judging and settling all the problems the people brought to him,
and nearly wore himself out.
But Jethro, our Father, was a lot older and more experienced,
and he knew God well enough to understand what was going on.
He took Moses on one side and gave him some sound advice,
something about how to organise matters,
delegating the routine business to others,
only dealing with the real awkward ones himself.
That seemed to work out much better.
There were some good men amongst the Israelites,
Once they got the idea that they were free men,
and could come forward.

Anyway they soon all setout on their travels,
I understood they were going to Canaan,
But I know they went first to the holy mountain,
and from what I heard, Moses met with God again there,
and God gave the people some written laws on stone tablets.
That's only rumour here,
You will need to speak with someone who was there to get the facts.
I haven't seen them since that time.
The last I heard was that they were still in the desert country.
Building up their strength and stamina I suppose
because they would not get into Canaan without a fight.
Zipporah and her son Gershom went with them.
We haven't seem them since, either.
It all seems a long time ago, but we still miss them here.
I hope they managed to live up to all the ideals Moses had for them,
and that they found a new permanent home.
That's what they all seemed to want most of all.

CHAPTER TWO

God Incarnate

CHAPTER TWO • *God Incarnate*

Advent

ST MARY S BILLINGSHURST 29TH NOVEMBER 1992

OUR *advent hymn is an appeal to our Lord to come, and we sing it as we prepare to celebrate His coming. Yet we know that He has indeed come, and He will not come in that way again. His next coming will be in glory and in judgement, and this world as we know it will have come to its appointed end. Why then should we ask for that which has already taken place?*

That is how the mind of a worldly person with some small knowledge of Christianity might work. The more discerning and spiritual person may well know that in our celebration of the event of that coming there is both a deep need and a profound reality. God has come to us in Christ, yet that coming can grow stale, can so easily become just a part of the background scenery of our minds. We need the renewal of that coming, the revitalisation of our faith and of our knowledge of Him, and we need the new life that He alone can offer to us. The profound reality is that as we celebrate the coming of our Lord, and the events of His life, His death and his glorious resurrection, and in that celebration open ourselves to His presence, He does indeed come again. Just as when we remember Him in the Sacraments, the remembrance is not just patterns of words, it is something that calls the events of history into new life, and brings His presence to us in a reality we can know. So it is also in all our celebrations of His life. When we recall the coming of our Lord, looking back on the events and their meaning as we interpret them through the words of prophecy and through our understanding of history, these events come to life again in our hearts; our Lord can truly come again to us and fill us once more with that light of life which He alone can bring.

Come to us Lord,
Come as a living sign,
Emmanuel, God with us.
Your people of old turned away from you,
Their enemies took them far from home,
to the loneliness of Babylon.
Yet you forgot them not.
You drew them with cords of love
and brought them again to your Holy City.
We too know how easily the world can tempt us from your presence,

and lead us into dark places.
Come, Lord Jesus, come
and ransom us afresh from our captivity.

Come to us, Lord.
Come as the Son of Jesse came to Your people of old.
We recall how he threw down the giant
with stone and sling, wielded in God's name.
For we live today in a world of giants,
powers of evil that seek to enslave us.
And we know our weakness.
Come to us again, Lord,
Fill us with your strength,
and defend us from evils which are too strong for us
Come, Lord Jesus, Come.

Come to us, Lord.
Come as the light which pierces and overcomes all darkness,
Shine upon us as we dwell in this land of deep darkness.
Come as the Prince of peace and bring peace to the warring souls of men.
Come as the Counsellor, that justice may prevail.
Bring the light of eternal life into our hearts
and banish our fears.
Come, Lord Jesus, Come.

Come to us, Lord.
Come as the King who can guide and lead His people
as David led Your people of old
making them a great nation.
For we are divided and uncertain.
not knowing which way to go
or which voice to hear,
and we make little progress in life.

CHAPTER TWO • *God Incarnate*

Unite us, Lord, behind Your banner
Write Your law of love upon our hearts, That we may walk in Your ways,
Ways that lead us out of darkness and misery,
and into the light of Your kingdom.
Come, Lord Jesus, Come.

Come to us, Lord.
Come in all Your Glory
and fill the world with Your majesty and power
that all may bow before You,
and all may know in truth that You are God.
Come again as You have come before,
for though we stand in fear before You
we long for the day of Your coming,
that day when all evil shall be banished
and there shall be a new heaven and a new earth.
Come, Lord Jesus, Come.
Amen.

'Where are You, Lord?'

A MEDITATION *for the Advent Season*

Where are You, Lord?
Where must we turn to find You
Where do we go to comprehend You?
I go out into the night and look upwards to the heavens,
to see the patterns You have woven amongst the stars.
Patterns of light, some brilliant, some faint,
Designs in colours of white, red, blue and yellow,
and millions more too faint for the eyes to see.
And I know that some of the light which reaches my eyes,
has been travelling across vast realms of space for thousands of years;
Distances far greater than I can comprehend.
In the majesty of the Universe we see Your Glory, Lord,
and we worship You.
But we cannot comprehend You.
The Creator and sustainer of all this vast expanse
in which our whole world is only as a speck of dust,
is too great for our minds to encompass.
We cannot find You in that Glory, Lord.

I wait for the day to dawn.
for the vision of the Heavens to fade in the light of the sun,
and I look upon the world which You have made.
And that too is a place of wonder, Lord.
I see the beauty and variety of living things.
The power and the fury of the seas,
with storm driven waves crashing upon the beaches in sheets of flying foam.
Amid the howling violence of the wind.
I see the grandeur of mountain ranges

CHAPTER TWO • *God Incarnate*

thrusting their snow-capped peaks up through the clouds.
The silence of frozen polar wastes,
and the burning heat of the desert sun.
In the strength and beauty of nature, Lord,
we see Your power
And we worship You.
But the power is too mighty for us to comprehend.
Few of us can climb the mountain
or conquer the power of the sea,
or live in the extremes of heat and cold.
None of us can create life as You have created it.
And we fear to approach Your power
lest we be destroyed by it.
We cannot find You in that power, Lord.

I turn to the world of men and women, Lord.
To the world portrayed in our newspapers,
and on our television screens.
I hear sounds of gunfire,
reports of violent deeds,
of cruelty, of callous disregard of life and liberty.
There is greed on every side.
There is distrust and hatred between different ethnic groups,
and people living in fear along the borders.
Where are You, Lord?
How can we find You amidst all this evil?

Look again upon this world around you
A world preparing for a holiday,
a celebration.
I see lights and pictures on all sides.
The busy shops resound with familiar music.
The magazines are filled with suggestions for expensive gifts.

CHAPTER TWO • *God Incarnate*

But I cannot see You, Lord, in all this tinsel,
nor hear Your word amid the jingling bells.
Until, in a window, there is a picture
A baby on a straw filled bed,
watched over by angels,
adored by shepherds and worshipped by Kings.
Here is a presence I know, a miracle I understand,
for I have been a part of it.

Here the glory of Creation shines out in a humble dwelling
and all the power of nature is contained in a human frame.
Here, Lord, You have come to us as one we can comprehend,
in a frame our arms can enclose,
with power limited to that which our minds can encompass.
And it is a sign to us,
a sign which always points us to Your presence,
For You are present within us.
Your incarnation hallows our humanity
even though we may disgrace it.
In our hour of need we look not at the glory of the stars,
or at the power and strength of nature,
but within ourselves
and within each other
And there, in the power of Your love,
We find You.

Look again at the world,
with all its evil and pain.
Now we can see You, Lord
standing alongside all those who suffer,
lifting the burden from those who are heavy laden,
comforting, by Your presence, all those who grieve or are distressed.
We see Your presence in those who minister to the needs of others,

and in those who receive ministry,
and we hear a voice saying
'Inasmuch as you have done it to one of the least of these, my brethren,
you have done it unto me'.

Lord, when we are overcome by Your Glory,
or we tremble before Your power,
Help us always to remember that You have come to us in our weakness
and shared our life,
and our death,
and that You are always with us
in the very depth of our being.
Help us to hold fast to that great loving presence,
and, as we hold fast,
help us always to seek to share that love with others around us in the world.
For we know that this is Your will for us,
and we ask it in the name of Him who came to us,
who comes to us still,
and will come for ever.
Jesus Christ our Saviour.
Amen.

God Comes in Christ

WE HAVE a story of Creation;
The Word of God at work,
Forming a world and a people for Himself.
A world of great peace and beauty
and a people fit for companionship with their Creator.
But the people were not strong enough for their task,
though they believed otherwise.
They were not content to live in the strength of God,
or in the understanding of His wisdom,
They listened to temptation
And sought to possess the wisdom of God Himself,
that they might go their own way,
and take possession of the world which God had made,
holding it for themselves.
And in so doing
mankind created the rift of sin,
the great barrier between themselves and God.
A snare of great strength from which they could not break free.
And God was sad.

But God did not give up on His world
or on His people.
He sought them again in love.
There was a chosen group
a small nation,
people who had been brought to know their weakness and inadequacy
by the power of oppressive government
and strong armies.
A helpless people
who cried to God in their weakness,

CHAPTER TWO • *God Incarnate*

though they did not know to whom they cried.
And God heard their cry
and put forth His power
to overcome their enemies
and rescue them from their foes.
He delivered them into a rich and fertile land,
and called on them to serve Him,
and to serve the people round about.
To be a light to the nations,
a light that would guide them back to Himself.

But again, the people failed Him.
New generations arose who turned their backs on the Lord,
going after the gods of the nations
in whom was no power at all.
They trusted instead in the power of political alliances,
and in the strength of uncertain allies.
The call for justice was loud in the land,
but it was not heeded.
And once again the nation was overcome,
and the people felt the yoke of the oppressor on their shoulders.
And in their time of trial they called again to the Lord.
Begging that He might rend the heavens and come down
to free them from their misery and distress.

Our God is faithful
and His steadfast love will never fail.
Even when His people turn away, he loves them still.
His Word has still its ancient power,
and when the time is right, He speaks.
The heavens were rent
And God Himself came down to earth.
Not in the power of fire or tempest,

CHAPTER TWO • *God Incarnate*

nor in the might of armies,
but in the power of love,
love contained in the weakness of a child.
There was a lesson for the nations
in the failures which had gone before.
The power of armies,
the majesty and authority of the law
were not the ultimate things.
Before them, the nations trembled,
but, trembling, they still went wrong,
still pursued their own ends to ultimate disaster.
And even God could not prevent them by such means.
For the true power of God does not reside
in earthquake, storm or fire.
Or in the power of armies. The evil one can use these things also.
And so often men turn towards darkness rather than light.
But in the power of love is made perfect in weakness.
And in that still small voice the Word of God is heard.
The love that shone through a tiny child,
was sufficient to bear the burdens of the world,
and to overcome the power of sin and death
for ever.
Evil cannot use that power, and cannot overcome it.

The pattern repeats itself in our lives.
So often we turn from God,
believing that we are strong enough for the tasks of life,
when we are not!
Believing that we can make a life for ourselves,
in our own way.
Only to find that that way takes us far from God.
And there is no future in it.
But God in Christ comes not just once to this world.

CHAPTER TWO • *God Incarnate*

He comes where anyone calls
and stands at their side,
supporting their weakness with His strength.
Leading them along the paths of life and restoring their souls.

Lord, come to us again at this Advent season.
Shine on our lives with the light of Your love;
Show us those dark corners and those empty areas
where we have turned away from You.
Speak to us through the lessons of the past,
that we might learn from them
and apply them to ourselves,
and in the light of those lessons turn again to You for our healing.
Take from our shoulders the yoke of sin and the reins of self-will
and fit us instead with the hardness of love,
love shown to us in a little child:
love portrayed to us upon a cross:
love triumphant amongst us in the power of the resurrection:
love that suffers all things, yet never ends!
Come, Lord Jesus, Come!
Renew us once more, and fill us with Your love,
That we might have abundant life in You.
Amen.

And Kings Will Come

BILLINGSHURST, 5TH JANUARY 1992

IN THE *season of Epiphany we remember the coming of the Magi to the Baby Jesus. The readings from Isaiah and Revelation set for today both speak about the coming of Kings. But they span a vast period of time, from some 500 years before Christ to the vision of the second coming at some indefinite time in the future. I have been thinking about these readings and this particular season, and have called this meditation, 'And Kings shall come!' a quotation from Isaiah.*

Jerusalem, City of David.
Home of Kings, and the place where God's name was placed.
The Temple, the very house of God,
A place of prayer and sacrifice,
a place that was filled with the Glory of God for those with eyes to see.
All is ruined, dead,
a place of darkness and despair.
The Temple is a heap of burned stone,
The city walls are broken,
the gates are choked with rubble
and the people are gone.
Even the voice of prayer is silent.

But a light dawns in the darkness.
The exiles return with high hopes.
The temple site is cleared.
The voice of the prophet resounds through the streets,
summoning the people to greater efforts.
Jerusalem, you shall again be great,
Shining with the Glory of the Lord,
And Kings will come to the brightness of your rising
bearing gifts and praising God.

CHAPTER TWO • *God Incarnate*

But the people cannot catch the vision,
their strength is inadequate for the task,
and they have forgotten the Lord, the source of their strength.
The light flickers and grows dim.
Kings do come, but they bear swords, not gifts.
They come for conquest, not for praise.
And there is suffering where there should be hope,
pain where there should be joy,
hatred where love should reign.
The true light would come again when God was ready,
but not before.

That light did come,
not to the mighty city but to nearby Bethlehem.
The light of the Glory of God was seen in the heavens,
and concentrated in a manger.
Kings came, bearing gifts,
just as the prophet foretold,
But the gifts were tokens,
and the City could neither understand nor accept.
The Gold of kingship was spurned,
the purity of Frankincense was ignored,
Only the bitterness of Myrrh could they bring to reality,
And the glory of God shone forth from a tree.
The light was bright for those who could see,
But the city was dark.
It drove out the light,
and in the darkness, died once more.
The Kings had come,
But they had not stayed.
Only God stayed,
watching, sorrowfully, over his erring children.

CHAPTER TWO • *God Incarnate*

Yet, even as the City died, it was being reborn.
There is a New Jerusalem, coming down out of heaven,
coming from God.
And all that is good is being drawn into it.
The world cannot see clearly
for the light of the Glory of God is dimmed in this world.
Only those who see the face of God in Jesus have light to see by,
and many have turned from that light.
But that light will come again,
with a brilliance such that none can turn away from it.
The darkness will be no more.
And Kings and Queens will lead their people into that city
carrying the glory of the nations,
Their gifts will not be tokens only,
they will be real gifts for the King of Kings,
For all good things will be part of His dominion,
By His light will the nations walk
and all evil shall be swept away.
And of this light there shall be no end,
for darkness shall be no more.

Lord, we look for the day of Your coming,
We look for the light that will lead us to Your New Jerusalem.
Help us to walk by the light that You have given, and lead us to that greater light.
Take us and mould us as You would have us be,
that we might be found worthy to come into Your city
bearing our lives as gifts fit for the King of Kings;
that we might become part of that glory
and dwell in Your wonderful light for ever.
Amen.

CHAPTER THREE

Christ's Life and Work

CHAPTER THREE • *Christ's Life and Work*

The Calling of the Disciples

BILLINGSHURST 7TH FEBRUARY 1993

A FEW *weeks ago we were thinking about the calling of Peter by Jesus, as it is described by St Luke. However, scripture does not give us a single unequivocal picture of this event, and indeed this is true for many other events also. Each evangelist seems to have selected those particular aspects of the Gospel story which seemed to him to be most important for the conveying of the truth which God wished to be conveyed to us who read their work many years later. And when we try to fit the different accounts together we run into very real difficulties, difficulties which are compounded by the fact that different people sometimes appear to have historical events in a different order. We need to remember that the Gospels were not written down until many years after the events described, and by the time they were being written it was the meaning and significnce of the events which wre more important to the writers than their historical order. Their purpose was to answer the request, 'We would see Jesus', a request which is today, and will remain for ever, one of paramount importance to all humanity. For it is in seeing Jesus that we see the Father at work in His Kingdom.*

But having said that, there remains the possibility that by fitting together the various accounts, filling in the details through the hints and suggestions that are contained in them and allowing space for things which might have been omitted, we will be able to see a little more of Jesus than the individual evangelists were able to reveal. And so I have tried to do just that for these accounts of the calling of the disciples tonight. For this purpose I address the question, 'Just what really happened at that time?' to Andrew, for he seems to have been the first contact among the twelve. And perhaps this is what he might have answered.

You mean that time when jesus called us to follow Him,
down by the lakeside where we were fishing?
No, that wasn't the first time we had seen Him
or listened to Him speaking.
It was a bit of a shock when the call came through.
We were, in a sense, waiting for something like that to happen,
but when it did there was no warning,
just a bit of preaching about the time being fulfilled,
and then the call.

CHAPTER THREE • *Christ's Life and Work*

It was instant decision time for us,
but we all knew there could only be one decision.
If the time was right, then it was time to go,
and we went!
But it had all begun quite a long time before
when John, the Baptist, not Zebedee's son, had started his mission,
preaching the need for repentance and baptism.
He was working far down the Jordan near Jerusalem.
Peter and I had gone to hear him, and had been baptised in the Jordan
and we remained with John for a while as his disciples,
while we tried to understand the trouble that was coming,
and the sinfulness that was bringing it about.
Then Jesus came to John for baptism.
We did not see what happened, we were a little way away,
talking to another group.
Afterwards, the people told us that John had not wanted to baptise him,
that he had said something about Jesus baptising him instead,
but Jesus had insisted.
And then, when he came up out of the water, there was a voice from heaven,
and something like a dove which came down upon him,
only it was no ordinary dove,
and the voice was the voice of God.
And John said to us afterwards that Jesus was the holy one of God
the lamb who was to take away the sin of the world.
We were intrigued, but we found it all a little hard to believe.

It was some time before we saw Jesus again,
but one day John pointed Him out to us,
and repeated to us that this was the Lamb of God.
And we felt we had to find out more about it all,
so we followed Him, and spoke with Him for some days.
Then He spoke of returning to Galilee,
and as we hadn't been home for some months, we went with him.

CHAPTER THREE • *Christ's Life and Work*

In Galilee my friend, Philip brought His friend Nathanael to Jesus
and he joined our company.
We went to a wedding in the next town together
and jesus was approached when the wine ran out
as if He was expected to do something about it.
Perhaps He did, for suddenly there seemed to be plenty,
but the only thing I remember clearly was something he said to Mary, His Mother
something like, 'my time is not yet come'.
We were to hear things like that quite often over the next few weeks.

Jesus went back to Jerusalem soon afterwards, for the Passover,
and then He went with some of us to join John.
We helped with the work of baptising,
but Jesus seemed content to talk with people,
and with us.
He told us something about the time when he went away
He went into the desert to be alone.
He knew now that He belonged to God in a special way,
and that He had a great work to do,
and great powers to do it with,
but He was not yet sure how to go about the task.
He knew that the ideas that had come to Him in the desert were wrong,
They were not God's ideas at all.
And while the work that John was doing was a good start,
it was not showing people the true nature of God,
For He knew that God was a God of love,
who cared for His people even when they were going wrong.
But He was awaiting a sign from God that it was time to start something different.
To preach that new message of God's forgiving love.
And we were waiting too,
even while we went on with the work that John was doing.
We knew that great changes were in the offing,
but we didn't understand quite what might be about to happen.

Some time later Jesus suggested that we return to Galilee.
Some of us went ahead, eager to see our homes again,
and He said that He would meet us there.
He was to say this to us again much later on,
and in a very different context,
and it was right, both times.
So we went, and returned for a while to our fishing.
But it was only for a few weeks.
Then word came that John had been arrested,
and almost immediately Jesus appeared on the sea shore.
He seemed to be almost a new man,
on fire with a message, like a man filled with the Holy Spirit,
and a great crowd were following, and listening to His words.
And those words were indeed full of fire.
'The time is fulfilled, The Kingdom of God is at hand'.
John had said many times that something like this was coming,
but Jesus said 'It's here, now!'
And we thought, 'This is what we have been waiting for,
This is the word that must be spoken'.
And I wondered if He would want us to go with Him,
whether He would still need us
or indeed whether He would allow us to be with Him.
I know that I desperately wanted to follow Him
for there was so much more that I wanted to know.
But then He came up to us.
'It's time', He said, 'Come with me now, and I will make you fishers of men!'
We didn't understand that at the time,
but we knew that there was nothing we wanted more than to find out.
So without more ado, we packed up the gear, and went with Him.
And the rest you know.
It has not always been easy,
but we have never regretted that decision,
for it has brought us great joy and a deep peace,

CHAPTER THREE • *Christ's Life and Work*

the knowledge that we are doing God's work and are safe in His care.
And we know that that will be true also
for everyone else who will tread this same road.
And we rejoice and give thanks to God for all he has done for us,
in Jesus.

The Gift of New Wine

'YOU have kept the best wine till the last' was the cry at the feast
But the stewart knew neither what the best wine was,
nor from whence it came.
It was not yet time for him to read the sign as it was given.
But did You, Lord, know even then,
what the new wine would really be?
Did you know then, right back at the beginning,
the grapes from which that new wine would be trodden?

But of course it wasn't the real beginning.
That had happened long ago.
'Before Abraham was, I am' were your words.
When the dry land appeared from the water. You were there.
The water,
that in its proper place was to become the water of purification.
The route by which men were to strive to lift themselves to heaven,
The means by which we sought to rid ourselves of the stain of sin,
and we could not.

The purification became the cleansing by baptism,
the sign of repentance,
But this too was no more than a preparation.
of no real effect on its own.
The water of cleansing had itself to be transformed,
changed into the wine of salvation.
And this was the sign of its changing.
The new wine so good that nothing before it could compare.
New wine for new people,
and for new ways.
Too much of a strain for old wineskins.

CHAPTER THREE • *Christ's Life and Work*

But this wine is different,
It can renew the wineskins itself, it we so will.
It can repair the tears and restore the blemishes
making old vessels altogether fit for new purposes,
vessels cleansed by the water of purification
can overflow with new wine
so that all the people may rejoice.

Lord, we remember from whence this new wine comes.
'I am the true vine, the fruitful vine.' are your words.
But the fruit of the vine was crushed in the winepress,
that the wine may flow forth.
'This cup is the new covenant in my blood,
shed for all for the forgiveness of sins.'
These too are Your words, and these too we remember
Precious wine, infinitely valuable,
Not to be wasted or lost
Must it then be kept only for a few?
Those who know its value?
'The steward knew not from whence it had come.'
and neither did the guests,
Yet all drank with rejoicing.
Locked away in the jars it was just water,
Good cleaning living water from the spring of life,
but water still.
Drawn off and shared out, it was rich wine,
Wine fit for a King,
For it was a King who provided it.

Lord, grant to us to share truly in this new wine,
this wine in which You come to us Yourself.
Grant to us that we may know the real riches which it brings
The salvation which is the free gift of grace.

That as we lift the symbols from Your table,
We may see the reality that is present in them.
And grant too that we may not seek to keep these gifts to ourselves,
but that we should freely share them with all who will listen,
That all the world may come to You,
Come to that great Love so wonderfully manifested to us
and be refreshed and renewed
by the inexhaustible resources which You offer,
and be filled with the new wine of Your spirit.
Amen.

CHAPTER THREE • *Christ's Life and Work*

The Man who was Born Blind

HOW could I ever forget that day
It was a day of wonder,
a day which changed every part of my life for ever.
Every minute of it is as clear to me now as it was when it happened.
And yet it started just like any other day,
a long wearisome time with little to do.
I had spent 25 years of such days,
begging for a living
sitting at the roadside
in darkness.
I had never known what light was for myself,
only through the words of others.
But on that day everything was to be changed.
I was sitting in my usual place,
asking for favours from those who passed by;
I suddenly became aware that there were men around me,
discussing me,
asking each other why it was that I was blind.
And one of them said something very strange,
said it in a way which made me sit up, wide awake.
'I am the light of the world', was what he said,
And something about doing the works of the one who had sent him.
But it wasn't so much the words themselves
as the way He said them.
There was something about the sound of them
which cut through all the noise of the market place,
and it was as though there was a great stillness all of a sudden,
like the stillness that sometimes comes in the middle of a storm,
and I knew that something very strange was about to happen
and that it would happen to me.

50 DEREK JAMES MORRILL • *Meditations*

CHAPTER THREE • *Christ's Life and Work*

And then, all at once there were hands on my face.
Something sticky was smeared on my eyes.
Somehow I knew that it was all right
it was being done for me,
to bring me something good,
and my heart missed a beat or two.
Was it really possible . . . the only thing I really wanted,
I couldn't ask, it seemed that to ask would destroy that sudden hope.
But then he spoke to me.
'Go to Siloam and wash your face in the pool.'
There were no promises,
just that wonderful feeling that all would be well,
and just below that the dreadful fear that it wouldn't be.
I knew the way to the pool,
and I went there as quickly as I could,
feeling the way with my staff.
I plunged my head into the water
and scrubbed my face with my hands
keeping my eyes closed.
For a long while I dare not open them.
I longed to do so, but I was too frightened.
And then, at last, I opened my eyes,
and for the first time in my life I found out what seeing was about;
and it was so wonderful I did not know how to speak of it.
My staff was cast aside, and I ran home,
shouting my joy to all who would listen.
I was in such a state that even my friends hardly knew me.
I could see, I could see,
and nothing else in the whole world mattered.

But there was more to come.
some good, some bad.

CHAPTER THREE • *Christ's Life and Work*

A group of pharisees came marching down the street
They didn't sound very happy,
didn't share my joy at all.
It was a Sabbath day, and they did not approve.
Could there be a better day to receive such a gift?
But to them it was all wrong.
'Who did it?' they asked.
And that was a strange thing,
for I realised I didn't know the man at all.
I'd heard his companions call him by name.
Jesus it was,
But that was all I knew.
But the question made me think about Him.
What manner of man was He?
The answers that came to my mind were confusing,
perhaps unbelievable,
So I just gave them the bald facts
and kept the new thoughts to myself for a while.
'Where is He now', they asked
Their voices were cold and angry.
I had no idea, and I told them so.
They started an argument among themselves.
'This man is not from God, He doesn't keep the Sabbath!'
'How could a sinner do such things?'
The argument went on around me for a while.
I thought about all those answers which kept coming to me.
Suddenly one of the pharisees grabbed me, pulled me forward.
'Let's hear what you have to say about it,' he said.
'After all, it was your eyes he opened'.
'He is a prophet!' I said
and they all laughed!
and one said scornfully, 'I don't believe he ever was blind'.
But my parents wouldn't let him get away with that one.

CHAPTER THREE • *Christ's Life and Work*

Still they wouldn't believe.
'Come on', they said, 'Now let us have the truth of the matter.
We know this man must be a sinner'.
'All I know for certain,' I said, 'is that I was blind;
Now, I see.
Why don't you also become His disciples and learn to do the same?
Only a man sent from God could do such a thing'.
That was the last straw for them.
They went mad,
shouted and screamed.
I was of no account, but they were important people,
and I had dared to try and teach them something about God!
'Get out!' they cried, 'Get out and never darken the synagogue door again!'
And they threw me to one side and marched off.
I was still happy,
who wouldn't be with new sight.
There were so many things to see.
Things I had only guessed at before.
Yet I was puzzled.
Just what had happened to me, and how,
Who was this Jesus.
He had given me my sight,
it could only have been a gift from God himself.
I owed Him everything, yet I didn't even know who He was.
Then, while I was wandering around,
just looking at people and things,
and wondering about it all,
a man came up and spoke to me.
'Do you believe in the Son of Man?' he asked.
The question made me jump.
The Son of Man, the one who was to come?
The Messiah?
But it wasn't just the question,

DEREK JAMES MORRILL • *Meditations* 53

CHAPTER THREE • *Christ's Life and Work*

it was the voice,
the presence.
Surely this was the man whose voice I had heard in the darkness.
But I wanted to be sure.
Was this really the man?
So I hedged, asked a question to gain both time and knowledge.
'Can you show me who He is, then I can believe'.
He smiled, and it pierced me through
just like the way that first shock of the light had stabbed into my eyes.
'I am He', He said,
and I heard again the echo of those words,
'I am the light of the world'.
and I knew Him,
and I fell to my knees and worshipped Him.
I have worshipped Him and followed Him ever since,
and I will do so for ever.
For who can deny the light of God when it comes right into their life.

The Penitent Pharisee

EVERYBODY likes to hear a good story teller at work.
Listening to stories often makes one think,
it exercises the imagination
and takes you out of yourself.
A good story can show you that there are more aspects of life than you had thought.
But sometimes a story can be a bit of a shock.
It can show you something you didn't really want to know.
Something about yourself.
And once you have seen it life is never the same again.
I suppose that has happened to many people, but once it happened to me,
and that changed my whole life.
It was at the time when Jesus of Nazareth was preaching,
moving down the country towards Jerusalem,
drawing great crowds.
I was a pharisee.
I believed that God had called us to achieve salvation through purity,
through keeping the law,
and separating ourselves from those who didn't do so.
If only everyone could keep the whole law for just one sabbath
then perhaps the Messiah would come and liberate us.
But most people were not too interested,
and now we heard rumours that this preacher, Jesus, was encouraging them.
Really it was too bad.
The Messiah would never come while the land was full of sinners.
They ought to be cast out and rejected.
Then those of us who wanted better things might get somewhere.

We heard that Jesus was teaching in the next village,
so a few of us decided to go and hear for ourselves,
perhaps we could put him right on some things.

CHAPTER THREE • *Christ's Life and Work*

When we found him he was surrounded by people,
all listening intently.
He was talking about sinners who repented,
and of the joy in heaven when this happened.
Well there's nothing wrong in that idea,
but I like to see some solid evidence of repentance,
and there are the accepted procedures for purification,
and they should be used, even if they are expensive.
But of course there are some people who can never be forgiven,
enemies of the people; and of God – we can never associate with them again.

Suddenly I realised that Jesus had started to tell a story,
about a man with two sons.
One of them was always getting into trouble,
wouldn't be told what to do,
and when he was told, often did something different.
The other was a good lad,
hardworking, respected his Father,
tried to keep the law.
He resented the way his younger brother got away with things,
and often made this quite plain.
They were always arguing and shouting at each other.
Nothing very unusual about this
I know several families who might qualify.
Eventually the younger brother had had enough of all this.
'Give me my share', he said, 'and I'll make my own way'.
So they sorted out his share, and not long after he left.
His brother was quite pleased,
but his Father wept for him,
and kept watch in case he should come home.
I don't know about weeping if he'd been my son.
I might have watched,
but I'd be in two minds about welcoming him back after all that trouble.

and I've known people who would say, 'I have no son. My son is dead'.

But in the story the son did come back.
He was flat broke, not a penny left of all that money.
Things hadn't gone well for him at all.
He came home in rags, starving.
But his father recognised him a long way up the street
and ran to meet him.
Made a tremendous fuss over him.
Even arranged a feast of celebration.
How could anyone make such a fuss over a son who had broken up the family?
He'd done more damage than the tax collector.
He'd even spent time looking after pigs, eaten them too I shouldn't wonder.
His brother wouldn't recognise him,
wouldn't go in to the feast at all.
And I couldn't blame him.
But then Jesus said a strange thing.
In the story the father came out to speak with the older brother.
'You've been a good son', he said,
'you know that you will inherit the farm in due time.
There is no need for a special celebration for you.
But your brother here is different,
He was dead, and now he is alive again,
He was lost, and now he has been found.
Won't you come in and join us?'
But the brother would not.
And there was a new, an even deeper separation in the family.

And then, as He spoke, Jesus suddenly looked straight at us pharisees,
standing in a bunch at the edge of the crowd,
looking disapproving.
And that look struck me like a blow.
For I realised what the story was really about.

CHAPTER THREE • *Christ's Life and Work*

He had been speaking earlier of the Kingdom of Heaven,
He still was.
It was God who was the Father,
and His people who were His family.
And I was part of that story,
and in the story I was not going to get to the feast.
For I was that elder son,
and all my self righteousness, all my years of toil,
and most of all my separation from others
was a waste of time and effort.
The separation wasn't just separation from evil and sin,
it separated me from God as well.
There was God saying, 'won't you come in and join us?'
And I was saying, 'No, Lord, it would defile me,
I have never sat down with sinners.'
But the sinner who came home was feasting in the Kingdom,
and I was outside, in the cold,
and between me and my Father was a great gulf,
one which I feared to cross
but which couldn't be allowed to remain.
And the trouble was that I knew Jesus was right.
Here in this story He had shown me how the steadfast love of God works.
The law permits the separation, and even maintains it.
But the love reaches out over the separation.

It was decision time. It couldn't be put off.
I left my friends and pushed through the crowd towards Him.
He turned to greet me.
'Rabbi,' I said, 'Let me stay with you.
I would hear more about God and the Kingdom,
and about sinners called to repentance,
for I too would be a part of that Kingdom'.
And I felt that I too had come home,

and been welcomed by my Father.
I was separated no longer,
for I am now part of the family,
and would wish to remain so for ever.

Lord, keep us always within Your family
Do not let the power of sin,
or the power of pride and self-righteousness,
come between us and You.
Help us to see the power of Jesus,
constantly at work,
bridging those gulfs which separate us
and drawing us always into Your presence.
We ask it in His name.
Amen.

CHAPTER THREE • *Christ's Life and Work*

The Pharisee's Table

IT IS *a proverbial saying that the onlookers see most of the game. As we read the stories in our Bible one way in which we can seek to understand them better is to adopt this role of onlooker. In fact it is something which is almost forced upon us, but as we do so, we have to remember that in these incidents Jesus was speaking as much to the onlookers as to the principal characters. And so, as we look on, we also have to become involved, to take the stories to ourselves and take our place within them, to seek to find for ourselves what Jesus is saying to us. I am going to seek to look into the gospel story of the Pharisee's table through the eyes of one such onlooker, a Jew who was present at the time and who took Jesus' message to himself. We will call him Matthias. This is his story, told as he meditates on what was a most important day for him.*

Yes, I remember that dinner party.
I don't think I am likely to forget.
It was the day when I first began to understand the message Jesus was teaching.
I had heard Jesus before, and I felt that there was something different about Him
but I could not put my finger on it.
So much of what He said was just good honest Jewish teaching.
Perhaps more honest than what some of the more eminent Rabbis taught.
I sometimes think they studied too much for their own good,
trying to set standards which were beyond most of us,
standards which made us all failure.
I admit that usually they tried quite hard to keep to them themselves,
but they didn't always succeed.
Like Simon, the Synagogue leader.
He was always very strict with himself, and with others.
And on the whole, he did very well.
There wasn't much in the law that he broke.
The trouble with him was that he knew it.
He thought he was the best man in town,
and made sure we all knew it as well.
He used to boast that all the travelling preachers and teachers came to him.

CHAPTER THREE • *Christ's Life and Work*

'They know I am a good Jew', he would say,
'That is why they visit me when I ask them'.
But sometimes, particularly when he disagreed with them,
His hospitality was not so generous.
The food was usually good, but the common courtesies were overlooked.
Still it gave the opportunity for some of us to hear a visitor speak.
The house was always open on these occasions.
It was like that when Jesus came.
There wasn't much by way of welcome.
Jesus was shown to his place and the meal commenced.
But then this woman came in.
She seemed in a bit of a state,
all upset about something.
She went straight to Jesus' feet as he reclined at the table,
and she wept over them.
We looked, and wondered, but Jesus seemed to take no notice.
Most of us knew who she was of course,
there are few secrets in a small town.
She had entertained many different men, and made a living from it.
Most of the people standing around drew away from her.
Suddenly the air was filled with perfume.
I had been watching Simon's face
but when I turned round I saw the woman had let down her hair,
She was wiping Jesus feet with it, and anointing them with perfume.
I looked back to Simon.
It was easy to see what he was thinking
it was written all over his face.
'I don't think much of this fellow, He's no prophet'.
'What sort of prophet would let a woman like that touch him?'
'Shall I call the servants and have him run out of town as an imposter?'
But before he could speak, Jesus himself spoke.
I turned and could see that he was smiling.
He could see well enough too what Simon was thinking.

DEREK JAMES MORRILL • *Meditations*

CHAPTER THREE • *Christ's Life and Work*

'Simon', he said, 'I have a question to ask you, an important question'.
Simon kept his composure, but not without an effort,
'What is it, teacher', he asked.
'There were two people in debt', Jesus answered, 'both to the same creditor'.
'One owed 500 pence, the other only fifty, but neither could pay'.
'The creditor was sorry for them, and forgave them both'.
'Now which one would you say will love him more?'
Simon thought about this for a moment,
certain that there was a trap in it, but he couldn't see it.
So he gave the obvious answer, 'The one who owed the most'.
'That's right', said Jesus, and then the trap was sprung.
'You see this woman', he said, pointing to her.
That question didn't need an answer.
Simon had been glaring at her for the last 20 minutes.
And Jesus went on, 'I have come to your house, you invited me,
but you have given me no water for my feet, no kiss of welcome.
you haven't even anointed my head with oil.
But you've seen what she has done.
She has washed my feet with her teras and dried them with her hair.
She has kissed them, and she has anointed them with oil'.
Simon was beginning to look distinctly uncomfortable, but there was more to come.
Jesus went on.
'She has shown how great her love is, so I tell you that her sins,
many as they are, and I do know that, are all forgiven,
but he who is forgiven a little, loves little.
And then he turned to the woman and said,
'Your sins are forgiven. Go in peace, your faith has saved you'.
Simon was completely discomfited,
and there wasn't much more conversation.
Some muttered among themselves,
asking where Jesus got the authority to forgive sins.
I didn't hear much of it
I was too wrapped up in my thoughts.

CHAPTER THREE • *Christ's Life and Work*

What Jesus had said and done seemed like a brilliant new light to me.
For the first time I realised that the sort of goodness old Simon practised
was not the most important thing in the world.
I had heard Jesus preaching about God and His love,
telling people that they must love God too.
Now I had seen that love at work.
Not many people saw that woman slip out of the courtyard,
they were too busy looking at Simon,
or arguing amongst themselves.
But I saw her go, and I saw her face.
It was transformed.
There were still tears, but they were tears of happiness.
I made it my business to find out what happened to her after.
The transformation I had seen carried on.
She left her old profession for good and spent her time helping others.
And I knew that I too must change,
and must seek that same forgiveness at the hands of Jesus.
And now I know myself the truth of His teaching,
because I know now how much I, too, need God in my life,
to make it all worth while,
and to make it means something.
Thanks be to God for all that He does for us.

CHAPTER THREE • *Christ's Life and Work*

The Healing of Jairus' Daughter.

A DAY to remember? Yes indeed, a day of all days.
A day when disaster stared into our eyes and wouldn't go away.
Life had been good to me. I had served God and He had looked after me.
There was no shortage of money.
Our house was large and comfortable, with enough servants for our needs.
I was honoured in the community, elected as leader of the synagogue,
and there isn't much higher honour than that.
But we only had one daughter; God had not granted us any more children.
I don't know why, perhaps He thought one was sufficient.
She was the joy of our household, beautiful and friendly,
just twelve years of age and coming into womanhood.
We were arranging her wedding to the son of an old friend.
Then suddenly, this illness, bad, and obviously getting worse.
O we had the best doctors, not even King Herod had anyone better,
but it was no use, they would not do anything to cure her.
We were desperate
Then someone brought news that the man Jesus was back in town.
He had been turned out of the Synagogue
He claimed things that it didn't seem right for any man to claim.
But right or wrong, He was a powerful healer.
Perhaps He could help.
It was no good sending a servant to call Him,
This was too important a matter for that,
He might into have treated it seriously.
I went myself, wondering all sorts of things,
Would He come? there was that trouble in the synagogue last year,
Perhaps He would remember, and refuse to consider our trouble.
Could He help. He had cured many, I knew that, but some He could not cure,
some who would not accept His help, who did not believe in Him.
Could I trust Him enough? I did not know, I could only ask, even beg Him to come.

CHAPTER THREE • *Christ's Life and Work*

It was a hot and dusty day. No need to ask where He was.
There were hundreds of people pressing round Him.
Hanging on His words, asking for help.
They all knew me of course
My position in the town commanded respect, and a way opened.
I went up to Him.
I had thought to stand before Him and speak with Him, but I could not.
There was a presence about Him, a great stillness, a compassion,
and a sense of understanding.
I fell on my knees before Him.
'Jesus, help me, come and save my daughter's life'.
He smiled. 'Of course I will', He said.
'Stand up, and show me to your home'.
But the crowd still pressed about Him, and suddenly there was an interruption.
'Who touched me?' He asked.
What a thing to ask! In that crush He was finding it hard enough to keep His feet.
Suddenly there was this woman before Him
I knew her, she could not be approached, she was unclean because of her illness
But He touched her and spoke to her.
I did not hear the words.
'Why does He delay. My daughter is dying'.
The thoughts filled my mind and blotted out all else.

Suddenly I realised someone was pulling at my sleeve.
I was one of my servants.
'I am sorry sir', he said, 'It's too late, your daughter is dead.
Do not trouble the Master any more'.
Suddenly we seemed to be alone, the noise of the crowd faded.
All I could hear were those dread words.
'Too late. Too late. Your daughter is dead'.
But then, suddenly there were other words, cutting through that dreadful blackness.
'Do not fear. Only believe, and she shall be well'.
It was Jesus speaking again to me.

CHAPTER THREE • *Christ's Life and Work*

I do not remember that walk home, it was as if I were in a dream.
There was the noise of wailing and weeping,
suddenly it stopped.
A strong voice rose above it and cut it off.
I heard someone say, 'He says she isn't dead, and He hasn't even seen her.
I have seen the dead before, and I know what they look like.'
Then we were inside the house and the door was shut.
Inside all was peaceful.
There were just a few of us there, and my daughter lying on the bed.
Jesus went up to her.
He took her by the hand.
'Child arise'.
and then, a great stillness.
And as we watched, the colour rose up into her white cheeks.
She breathed. She opened her eyes.
And, wonder of wonders, she arose off the bed, and Jesus put His arms about her.
We stood there, paralysed with fear and joy and wonder,
unable to move.
Jesus turned to my wife and handed our daughter to her.
'Take her', He said, 'and give her something to eat, she will be hungry now'.
His words broke the spell.
We hugged our daughter, and my wife made haste to find food for her.
We didn't know what we could say to Jesus.
'Thank you' was nothing like enough.
We had seen the gift of God in action
right here, in our house, in our family.
But Jesus wouldn't let us do anything about it.
He even told us not to tell people about it.
'This is the work for which the father sent me into the world', He said.
'Give Him the thanks and the praise'.
And He left us and went on His way.
But His gift and our great joy remain with us.
Thanks be to God for the revelation of His love and power.

Lord God, help us to know our need of You.
Do not let pride, or self sufficiency stand between us.
Do not let worry and care bring a barrier.
Help us to come to You and ask for Your blessing in all life's difficulties.
Give us the confidence to be sure that when we ask, You will hear,
and that the power of Your love and care
is with us still, and will be for evermore.
Lord, hear our prayer, and keep us ever in Your love and care.
We ask it in Jesus name.
Amen.

CHAPTER THREE • *Christ's Life and Work*

The Stilling of the Storm

BILLINGSHURST URC 5TH JULY 1992

THE day that Jesus stilled the storm?
Yes I remember that all right.
None of us is likely to forget it.
It was that sort of day, a stupendous and frightening day,
particularly for me, for I am no fisherman.
I could pull a rope, or an oar if necessary
but I was never at home on the sea,
not in the way Peter and James and John and some of the others were.
And when that storm blew up and water started coming into the boat
I was scared stiff,
and with good reason, I think,
for we could see that even the fishermen were frightened by what was happening.
But if you want the whole story I should start from the beginning.

It had been a long day.
Crowds of people had been with us all day long
seeking to hear what Jesus had to say.
For part of the time He had been forced to stand in the boat
just a yard or two off shore
so that people could see and hear Him.
And at the end of the day He was tired
and we needed to get away from the people and rest, and have a meal.
So we set off to cross the lake to where there was a quiet spot.
It was quite calm when we set off, but even I know that can be deceptive.
The fishermen have many tales of the sudden storms which can blow up there.
They say it's something to do with the shape of the hills
and the direction of the wind.
Whatever its due to, it certainly happened that afternoon.
We hadn't got half way across when we saw the tell-tale patterns on the water,

and then suddenly the wind hit us and the waves began to build up.
The fishermen were struggling to keep the boat headed into the wind and waves
but despite their efforts, the waves were breaking over the side.
Then suddenly we became aware of something very strange.
Jesus was laying fast asleep in the stern of the boat,
resting on a pillow.
There was all this noise of wind and waves,
frightened men shouting instructions to each other.
The boat was bounding about on the waves,
yet Jesus was sleeping like a child,
just as if nothing was happening.
It seemed almost un-natural.
Surely He could help us.

Two of us made our way with difficulty down to the stern
in some danger of being thrown overboard,
and we roused Him.
Our near panic must have showed in our voices
as we shouted above the noise of the wind.
'Master', we said, 'the storm is too much for us,
we are in danger of sinking. Do you not care?'
He opened His eyes and looked at us,
and then stood up in the pitching boat,
raised his hand and spoke to the wind and waves.
'Wind, stop all this violence! Sea, be still, be at peace!'
He didn't seem to shout,
but His voice had a power and authority that we had not heard before.
And it penetrated the storm.
All of us heard it, even the man right up in the bow of the boat.
And the wind and the sea heard it too.
The screaming and the pressure of the wind died away
The wave tops flattened out,
and the boat stopped jumping about.

CHAPTER THREE • *Christ's Life and Work*

Suddenly, before we could understand what was happening,
we were sitting in silence,
rocking gently on a slight swell in the evening sunshine.
We were amazed, speechless, not knowing what to say or do.
Jesus turned to us and spoke again,
'Have you no faith? Why were you so afraid?'
There was no answer to that.
We had seen something happen that we believed only God could do.
We remembered what was written in scripture
about His wondrous works in the deep
shown to those who went out in ships;
'For He commanded, and raised the stormy wind,
which lifted up the waves of the sea.
They mounted up to heaven, they went down to the depths;
their courage melted away in their evil plight;
they reeled and staggered like drunken men, and were at their wits' end.
Then they cried to the Lord in their trouble,
and He delivered them from their distress;
He made the storm be still, and the waves of the sea were hushed.
Then they were glad because they had quiet,
and He brought them to their desired haven'.
We knew Jesus was special, that He was from God,
but this seemed to make Him equal with God Himself!
We were torn with conflicting emotions, fear, awe, and love.

Later we wondered even more
and one thing troubled us for a while.
Why did we have to ask for His help?
He was there in the boat with us, sharing the danger,
but He was sleeping.
Was He trusting in our ability?
That's a bit of a joke when we think about how things turned out.
There was no doubt now where the power and ability was.

But perhaps that is the way God wants to work with us,
He wants us to come to Him, to ask Him to deal with our needs,
before He can do what is wanted.
I wonder what would have happened if we hadn't asked Him that day?
But perhaps that is something we shall never be able to know!

Later we were even more puzzled when Jesus was arrested.
With power like that couldn't He have scattered a few priests
and a couple of dozen guards to the four winds?
I guess He could have done, but He chose not to.
We knew later that He had another battle to fight and win,
against a greater enemy entirely,
and the arrest was no more than the introduction,
the way which He had to follow.

Many years later Matthew was to remind us of this day.
It was a time of trouble when many of our friends were arrested.
We were expecting the same for ourselves.
Was this a time for a rescue,
or was it a lead in to a greater task.
We had to ask!
And we found that Jesus and His power were with us still.
Our church survived, although not without fear and suffering
But as soon as we asked, we knew that presence,
and we knew the calm that He brought.
It was a good lesson
One I will not forget.
We have a destiny within the purpose of God,
A purpose which Jesus came to tell us about
and to put our feet on the pathway.
And if we trust Him, if we are ready to ask for His help,
He will ensure that we will be able to fulfil that purpose,
whatever storms may suddenly assail us.

CHAPTER THREE • *Christ's Life and Work*

Thanks be to God for His power and His steadfast love shown to us in Jesus.
Amen.

CHAPTER THREE • *Christ's Life and Work*

The Thoughts of Nicodemous

BILLINGSHURST 7TH JULY 1991
EDITED FOR PETWORTH 8TH SEPTEMBER 1991

IT WAS a year or two ago when we first began to hear stories about Jesus.
Stories of miracles,
Of people being healed.
Even some who were lepers.
And demons being cast out and people made whole again.
But my fellow pharisees were not at all impressed.
'There are many stories of miracle workers', they said.
But I was intrigued
because there were other things being said as well;
This man wasn't just a healer,
He was also a teacher.
One who taught profound thoughts in simple stories.
And I too was a teacher;
a teacher of the law,
and people used to reckon I was quite good at it,
but here was someone who seemed to have something new to say.
Some, a few at least, of my colleagues also became interested.
For a while they went to hear Him speak.
Sometimes they would argue with Him.
But then word got around that Jesus did not keep the law.
Worse than that, He was saying that the law was sometimes wrong,
and shouldn't be kept.
Sometimes there were things which needed to be done on the Sabbath
and this was all right!
And there was more.
He neglected the rules about ritual cleanliness,
and he associated with sinners.
My colleagues became horrified.

CHAPTER THREE • *Christ's Life and Work*

The last straw was when he claimed to forgive sins.
'He's making himself equal to God!', my friends said,
'And that's blasphemy'.
But was it so?
Or was He speaking simple truth?
It didn't sound like blasphemy when you heard Him say it.
I was beginning to have some doubts about the law myself.
Even as I taught it to students.
Once it had been thought possible to keep the law in all its detail.
And we believed that if all Israel could only do that,
even if it was only for just one Sabbath,
then the Messiah would come.
It was an inspiring hope,
or was it perhaps only a dream?
Could anyone ever actually keep the whole law?
In every little detail?
It had begun to look unlikely to me.
It got harder and harder to do
and although I tried, I knew I could not manage to do it.
Perhaps we weren't on the right path after all.
Perhaps this new man had some ideas which contained a greater truth.
And certainly the miracles he performed seemed to have the hand of God in them,
whatever my colleagues said about them.

I thought about all this for a long time.
I had to be careful.
If I lost my position as a teacher,
and my reputation as a lawyer,
life would become very difficult.
I could not go openly to question him,
so I decided to go by night
and seek a private conversation with him.
Perhaps then I could make a clearer judgement.

When we met, Jesus seemed to know at once who I was,
and what I wanted.
I had heard others speak of His depth of understanding and knowledge of people
But I hadn't quite expected it to happen with me
and I was surprised.
I greeted Him as a teacher
and straightaway He started to speak to me of salvation
answering the question that was unspoken in my mind.
He spoke of being born again.
I understood something of what we meant,
that kind of language was familiar amongst teachers.
But I wanted to hear more
so I took the answer as a literal one, an impossibility,
and played it back to him.
And Jesus went on to speak of the things of the Spirit and of the flesh.
I pretended not to understand,
but Jesus was not taken in.
He knew how much I understood, perhaps also how little.
We talked for some time and spoke of many things.
He took me to task for the failure of us pharisees to believe his teaching
He claimed to have descended from heaven,
and spoke about being lifted up.
An ambiguous term that.
The Romans lifted people up on crosses.
A painful way of coming into God's presence.
But I thought that I understood much of what He said,
and there was a great deal to it,
but I couldn't accept it all.
Was this man actually the Messiah,
the anointed one we had all been waiting for?
That was where His words led,
and it was possible that He could be.
Although He wasn't the kind of man we had been expecting.

CHAPTER THREE • *Christ's Life and Work*

I couldn't be sure.
It was such a big step to take in my thinking,
and I wasn't ready for it.
I went away and pondered His words very deeply
but I kept them to myself.

There were many arguments with my colleagues over the following months.
I deliberately did not say too much,
I wanted to hear how others felt.
But when I weighed their words against His.
Their arguments did not seem to carry too much weight
and they were vindictive.
This was wrong, and I said so,
but they told me that it did not matter.
According to Scripture no prophet was to come from Galilee,
And I knew they were right on that.
It was only later that I found that Jesus was born in Bethlehem,
In accordance with the Messianic prophecy.
But by then other things had happened.
I had seen Jesus crucified,
and I thought it was too late.
I had come to believe that He was right.
I was on the point of going to Him again,
and declaring my belief
but now he was dead and it was all over.
I had confided in my good friend Joseph
and had found that He too had come to know, and to believe in Jesus.
We had talked together often in secret.
After the crucifixion Joseph came out into the open.
He begged Jesus' body from Pilate and buried it in his own tomb.
And I knew that I too would have to make a gesture,
To let people know just what I felt
even if it cost me my job.

So I went with him and helped with the burial.
It was a sad and difficult time,
for we didn't understand what was happening,
not until the third day.
Then suddenly all was made clear.
The tomb was empty and Jesus was alive.
Now I am no longer a teacher of the law.
I did lose my job, but it didn't matter to me at all,
for I know that the law is a dead word.
Instead I serve a risen and living Lord.
And the words of life that He spoke to me still vibrate in my ears.
For I know now that God so loved the world
that He gave His only Son,
that whosoever believes in Him shall not perish
but have eternal life.
I will give thanks to God for all my days for His great gift,
and I know that I will dwell with Him for ever.
Thanks be to God.
Amen.

CHAPTER THREE • *Christ's Life and Work*

The Faith of the Centurion

BILLINGHURST 6 OCTOBER 1991

HOW do we see that Centurion? What sort of man might he have been? The Centurions were the backbone of the Roman army, the equivalent perhaps to a Regimental Sergeant-Major. Barclay points out that wherever they are spoken of in the New testament, they are spoken of well, and he quotes from Polybius the historian, this list of the qualifications they needed. They must not be so much seekers after danger as men who can command, steady in action and reliable; they ought not to be over anxious to rush into the fight, but when hard pressed they must be ready to hold their ground and die at their posts. These are the kind of qualifications which denote men of outstanding character. I think that we may judge him to be a man of long experience, and one who had served many years in Palestine. He was clealry a man of some wealth, far beyond what he would draw as army pay, and one who was generous enough to be willing to spend that wealth for the benefit of others. Clearly too, he was a man of a genuinely religious nature, who had come to know God through his experience of Jewish religion, although, as a Gentile, he could only have seen that religion from the outside. He had probably seen and heard Jesus, probably on many occasions while He was living at Capernaum, and he had been able to recognise the extraordinary power and authority which was present in Jesus. So how might a man like that have told his story of that remarkable day, and of what had led up to it.

That was the sort of day no-one could ever forget,
the day I came to know the real power of God in the land.
There was my servant and friend, the man who had looked after me for many years,
lying on what was surely to be his death-bed
and then, the word of authority,
and his illness left him, and he got up, a fit man again.
It's not often you see something like that happen;
even less often that you can undersatnd how and why.
So I remember all right
I have spent hours thinking about it.
But perhaps we should start from the beginning.
You want to know how it was that a Roman officer should be involved like this,
how I came to ask that Jewish teacher for His help.

CHAPTER THREE • *Christ's Life and Work*

I come from a Roman family with estates not far from Rome itself
My family followed the celebrations of the Roman Gods,
but without any real enthusiasm.
There was an emptiness about it all,
a feeling that if there really were Gods like that they didn't count for much.
So we attended when we thought we ought to and enjoyed the feasts
and otherwise we went our own way.
As a young man in the army I was occupied with other things.
One had to concentrate and work hard at being a soldier.
Those who didn't were soon killed.
Fighting is not a children's game.
We saw life and death in plenty
and we concentrated on enjoying life while we could.
But as I got older I began to think more about the meaning of life
There must be some meaning beyond today's affairs.
And then I was posted to Galilee, to the permanent garrison there.
It was a long term posting, and a good one.
There was not much fighting to do,
only a few bands of robbers and zealots to deal with,
and we could settle down a bit,
get to know people.
I found some Jewish people who were a little less proud and stiff-necked than most
and got quite friendly with some of them.
We talked a lot about the meaning and purpose of life
and a lot of what they said made sense to me,
a lot more sense than the stories I had been brought up with.
They spoke of a God who had purpose,
a God who loved His people
and one who was unchangeable and steadfast.
And more than that, they knew where He had been active in the real world.
Their stories had a ring of truth about them,
thye were not just legends and fairy stories.
I felt that they had much to teach me.

CHAPTER THREE • *Christ's Life and Work*

They would not share my food, they had very strict rules about that
And of cousre I could not go into their synagogue
That was forbidden to those who were not born to their faith.
But I was permitted to go to the outer court,
and from there I could hear their teachers speak.
It was fortunate that I have something of a gift for languages
and I found it quite easy to learn enough of Aramaic, and even the ritual Hebrew to get by with.
The old Synagogue was in a bit of a mess, in fact it was falling down,
and my friends said they were having a problem with money to replace it.
They were mostly people with enough to live on, but no wealth in rserve.
I am no millionaire, but I am well provided for from the family estates,
and so I offered to help.
They were reluctant at first, but they needed the help
and so I put up much of the cash for that new building.
I felt good about that, felt that it was the right thing to do,
and it seemed that I got my reward in my increasing understanding of life
and of the Jewish teachings.

There was a lot in those teachings about the coming of a Messiah,
One who would liberate Israel and lead them into a new life.
It was difficult for my friends to talk much about this to me
although they soon ceased to see me as one of the oppressors.
But there was great excitement when we heard of this new teacher,
Jesus, they called him.
Clearly He was a man of some power.
He could heal the sick, and even demons obeyed him.
I had seen people possessed by demons and it was frightening at times.
But was He to be the Messiah?
My friends could not agree amongst themselves
and the discussions went on far into the night at times.

But then my servant fell ill.

CHAPTER THREE • *Christ's Life and Work*

I had the best doctors, but they could only shake their heads sadly and go away
'There is no cure', they said. 'Nothing can be done'.
'He only has a sort time to live'.
One of my Jewish friends asked me why I was so miserable looking,
so I told him what the doctors had said.
He thought for a bit, clearly wondering whether to say something or not.
Then he said, 'Jesus of Nazareth is in this area. I wonder if He could help?'
'But it wouldn't be right for me to approach Him', I replied,
'Besides I haven't heard of Him working for anyone who wasn't a Jew'.
'Don't worry about that', said my friend,
'You have done a great deal for us, and we'll send an official deputation to Him'.
And they did.
Then they returned and said Jesus was coming.

The next thing I saw was a crowd approaching the house,
and Jesus was with them.
I knew His face, for I had heard Him speak before.
I had stood at the back of the crowd beside the lake once or twice and looked on.
There was an air of authority about Him.
That was something I recognised, something I shared.
For when I spoke officially, when I was on duty,
all the authority of Rome was at my back.
But this was different.
This was an authority quite different from that of Rome.
And Jesus was heading towards my house,
a house He was not supposed to enter.
So I sent my friends to speak with Him again.
I told them to tell Him that I knew all about the working of authority,
that I was sure that if He would only speak the word
my servant would be cured.
There was no need for Him to come into my house.
Truth to tell, now it had come to this, I was frightened,
I, a Roman soldier, worried by a wandering unarmed preacher.

CHAPTER THREE • *Christ's Life and Work*

It sounds inconceivable,
But there was something about Him that I was afraid to face.
But then He turned to the crowd and spoke,
and He was near enough for me to hear Him.
He spoke of faith
and said that no-one in Israel had trusted Him quite like that.
He turned and smiled at me, and raised His hand,
and then they turned away,
and I heard my servant call out from the next room.
I ran to him, and found him well.

I am sure that God came to me that day,
that my long search for truth had been fulfilled in a person,
that I now had the beginnings of real understanding of life.
Since that time I have sought to find out more about Him,
I have heard His words again.
Since that time too, dreadful and wonderful things have happened.
Jesus was killed in Jerusalem;
killed by Roman hands.
I knew the officer on duty there that day.
He was only doing his duty, but it is still a hard thought to bear.
But it was not the end, for God raised Him again.
The tomb was empty, despite the guards.
And today I know that Jesus is still with me
just as He was on that day.
But today, I can welcome Him into my house
and into my life.
And I know that He will never leave me again.
Thanks be to God for all His goodness.

CHAPTER THREE • *Christ's Life and Work*

The Raising of Lazarus

THIS *story is told by Eleazar, a young man who lived at Bethany, a neighbour and friend to Lazarus and to Martha and Mary.*

I had lived in Bethany all my life,
so I knew Mary, and Martha, and their brother Lazarus, quite well.
I knew Jesus too, for He was often a visitor at their house.
They often asked me to help them, or to run errands for them.
One day Mary came to tell me that Lazarus was very ill.
He had been ill for several days, and was getting worse.
They asked me to go and find Jesus for them.
'It may be', Mary said, 'that He could cure my brother if He came'.
'But perhaps He will not come', I said,
'For His life was threatened when He was last here,
and He has gone across the Jordan for safety'.
Mary said, 'I know, but we must still tell Him. Will you go?'
Of course I went. You couldn't say no to Mary when she asked like that.
It was a good long day's journey, and I wasn't sure where Jesus was.
But I knew He was across the Jordan, so I set off towards where John used to preach.
I knew that He shouldn't be hard to find, and He wasn't.
As soon as I got anywhere near, people told me about Him.
So I soon found Him, and delivered my message.
And then jesus said a very strange thing.
'This illness is not unto death; it is for the Glory of God,
so that the Son of God may be glorified because of it'.
I didn't understand this, Lazarus had been pretty ill when I left.
He might even have died already for all I knew.
But Jesus did not explain.
It was now almost dark, so I spent the night with the disciples.
I knew several of them, and they talked to me.
'I don't know whether He will be able to come', they said,

DEREK JAMES MORRILL • *Meditations*   83

CHAPTER THREE • *Christ's Life and Work*

'The situation was definitely very dangerous when we last left'.
I thought of Mary's face, and I felt sad at this news.
She was counting on Him so much.
But I had a strong feeling that Jesus was going to do something,
although I didn't know what.

Next day I went back to Bethany, to tell Mary and Martha what was said,
but I found I was too late.
Lazarus was dead, and was being buried as I got home.
Mary and Martha were weeping unconsolably.
Many friends were with them.
I stayed with them for a while, and then returned to my home.
It must have been two or three days later that word came that Jesus was coming.
It seemed strange that He should risk His life now, when Lazarus was dead and buried.
I went to the house to see whether they had heard.
Mary was crying still, but Martha, always the more practical one, spoke with me.
'Yes, I know', she said, 'He's almost here. I am just going to meet Him'.
I went with her into the street, and suddenly Jesus was there.
She moved to greet Him,
and suddenly there was something different about her,
something expectant, a new hope.
She stood just that bit straighter,
as if her sorrow did not weigh quite so heavily upon her.
And yet she did not ask anything from Him,
But she said something quite strange,
something about God being willing to grant anything that Jesus asked of Him.
Jesus looked at her for a moment.
There seemed to be a strange silence on the street.
People were all around, but we seemed to be separate somehow,
isolated,
quiet.
'You know your brother will rise again', He said.
Martha replied 'Yes I know that he will rise again in the last day'.

CHAPTER THREE • *Christ's Life and Work*

Her voice was steady, quite devoid of emotion,
but there was a vast question in her eyes as she spoke.
Jesus put His hand on her arm, and spoke firmly and confidently.
'I am the resurrection and the life; he who believes in me, though he die,
yet shall he live, and whoever lives and believes in me shall never die.
Do you believe this?'
Mary looked at Him for a long moment. Then she spoke,
'Yes Lord; I believe that You are the Christ, the Son of God,
He who is coming into the world'.
They stood facing one another for several seconds.
Then suddenly the tension was broken.
Martha turned and went back toward the house.
I became aware once again of the people around us,
of movement,
of conversation.
But Jesus stood, silent.

I turned to follow Martha, thinking she might need me,
but I met her in the doorway of the house.
Mary was with her, and as I approached she ran into the street.
I saw Jesus coming towards her.
There were tears in His eyes as she fell at His feet.
He bent down and raised her up.
I could not hear what was said.
Then Martha touched my arm.
'Let us go to the tomb', she said.
Jesus and Mary were already moving that way.
We followed, and may of our friends also.
We were still sad, for sorrow is infectious among friends,
but we were strangely curious too.
There was a feeling in the air that something awesome might be going to happen.
Yet not everyone felt it.
Someone said, behind me, 'He should have come earlier,

surely He could have saved the man's life!'

We came to the tomb.
There was a great stone in front of it.
Jesus stood before it and said to us men 'Take away the stone!'
But we hung back, startled and doubtful.
Even Martha looked horrified.
She said to Him, 'Lord, it's been four days, there will be a foul smell'.
Jesus smiled at her.
'Martha', He said, 'Did I not tell you that if you would believe
you would see the Glory of God?'
She hesitated a moment and then, with sudden decision, said, 'Yes Lord',
and turned to the group of us standing near,
'Take away the stone! Open the tomb!'
We did as we were told and rolled away the great stone,
though it seemed a fearful thing to do.
Then we stood back.
jesus and the two women stood alone, near the tomb entrance.
We thought He would go in, but He didn't.
Instead He looked up to heaven and prayed.
I didn't hear the words properly,
Something about us seeing and believing.
The He spoke in a mighty, commanding voice.
The sort of voice that makes everyone jump.
'Lazarus! Come out!'
The words echoed down the hillside,
and then, as they died away, there was dead silence.
Everyone was holding their breath.
It seemed a long time, but it could only have been a few seconds.
Then there was a great gasp.
Something was moving in the darkness of the tomb.
Suddenly, there was the figure of a man,
all wrapped in grave clothes,

standing in the doorway.
For a moment nobody moved,
it was as though we were rooted to the spot.
Then Jesus spoke again, much more gently,
'Unbind him', He said, 'and let Him go'.
The words seemed to open the flood-gates.
The women rushed to help their brother and take him into the house.
Everyone was talking at once.
Some were praising God.
Others prostrated themselves before Jesus.
Mourning was turned into celebration on the spot.
The party went on for days.
And no one doubted that they had seen the power of God at work in Jesus.

It was a wonderful thing to have seen, to have been part of.
Something never to be forgotten.
But there was a price attached.
jesus went away again soon afterwards,
and stayed out of Jerusalem for some time,
but the next time He came, He was arrested and executed,
And someone told me that it was this miracle which finally caused it.
The authorities were afraid of losing control of the people because of Him.
So they did away with Him, or at least they tried to.
They might have known it was no use.
God had shown us His power over death.
And that went for Jesus as well.
Three days after his execution, the disciples told us He too came back to them.
Now we all know that He is alive, and with us for ever.
He really is the Resurrection and the Life.
Thanks be to God for all the wonders He shows to us.

CHAPTER THREE • *Christ's Life and Work*

Jesus Wept Over Jerusalem

BILLINGSHURST 7TH MARCH 1993

THE *things that Jesus did and said must often have appeared very strange to those who were looking on, and few of them were perhaps more strange looking than the events of this meditation. This was a time of celebration, a time when many people may have felt that here was the start of something big, something new in the world, a bit of real action on God's part after the a long period of depression. And suddenly, the chief figure in the procession, the one who seemed to be the centre of all the new hopes, stops and laments over the coming fate of the City, laments with tears in his eyes. Just what was happening, and what was going to happen? But then, equally suddenly the moment is over, and the procession continues. But for many there must have been a nagging doubt about it all, something not to be thought about, at least for the moment, but a memory that would return to haunt the onlookers many times in later years.*

I want to look at this incident through the eyes of one of the onlookers. Not a disciple, but perhaps a friend of Judas Iscariot, a patriot, possibly a supporter of the Zealot movement. Certainly one who wanted to see the Romans out, and who was ready at least to consider the use of strong measures to obtain this end.

My name is Baruch and I come from a village near Jericho.
I was brought up to hate the Romans,
My uncle was crucified by them as a rebel,
and my father never forgave them,
I would have joined the Zealots myself,
but my Father counselled otherwise.
'Wait', he said, 'It is not yet time, but the time will come.
Wait, but be ready. It might not be for too long,
Remember the words of the prophet, Zephaniah,
"The Lord your God is in your midst,
a warrior who gives victory".
and there are rumours that the Messiah is coming.
We hear of this man Jesus who has God given powers,
and many hope that He is the one who will save Israel'.

CHAPTER THREE • *Christ's Life and Work*

That counsel seemed good to me,
so I tried to find out more about this man Jesus.
I spoke with others who had seen and heard Him.
There seemed no doubt about His power
for some I spoke with had been healed by Him,
and others had been fed in a desert place.
But His message I could not understand, for He spoke of peace, and of loving enemies.
Rumour had it that He had even healed a Roman Officer's servant up in Galilee.
This seemed very odd, hardly the start of a revolution.

Then I met a man named Judas.
He told me that he was close to Jesus,
and he too had hoped for mower powerful action.
But he thought that perhaps the time wasn't quite right.
But he said also that Jesus was intending to go to Jerusalem for Passover,
and perhaps that would be when things would get going.
The Passover crowd could easily be turned into a mighty army
by a few suitable words at the right time.
In fact, he said, he was thinking about some action which might force Jesus hand.
He wouldn't say what it was, and I didn't question him;
it seemed unwise to do so.
He was a big strong man with slightly wild eyes,
and I thought he was carrying a weapon under his clothes.
But I thought a lot about what he had said.

A few days later I heard that Jesus had passed through Jericho
and was on His way to Jerusalem.
I pushed some food into a bag and hurried out to see if I could find Him.
It wasn't difficult, there were many others doing the same thing.
As we walked along with the growing crowd towards Bethphage
the excitement was building up.
People were asking each other.
'Is this the day? Are we going to see the Romans thrown out at last?'

The crowd got thicker, and more excited.
Suddenly I saw Jesus.
Someone had found a donkey and set Him upon it.
People were shouting and cheering and waving branches.
Some were even spreading their cloaks in the road for Him to ride over.
The crowd came over the crest of the Mount of Olives
and commenced the long descent towards the Kidron valley and Jerusalem.
I was caught up in the excitement and shouted and danced with the others.
As we came in sight of Jerusalem, I was not far from Jesus.
I was looking towards the City and the Temple
when suddenly the shouting died away.
We turned to see why, and there was Jesus, standing beside the donkey.
He appeared to be weeping; there were tears on his cheeks.
And suddenly He cried out.
'Oh Jerusalem, would that even today you knew the things that made for peace'
and He went on to speak about the city being attacked and destroyed,
all because they did not know the time of their visitation.
It was very strange.
All the crowd that had been shouting so loudly were silent,
disturbed, even horrified by His words.
Was this the start of the glorious revolution?
A cloud moved across the face of the sun,
and we shivered in the sudden chill,
but the chill was something more than just a brief shadow.
It was as though a moment of tragedy had entered into the festivities.
But the moment passed, the cloud moved away, the sun shone again,
and Jesus remounted his donkey and continued towards Jerusalem.
And the people cheered again,
although it was some time before they matched the previous intensity.

In Jerusalem, another strange thing.
Jesus went to the Temple and drove out the traders.
No one much minded about that except the high priest of course,

CHAPTER THREE • *Christ's Life and Work*

they had grown rich from their extortions over the years,
and the priest with them,
but it was our money they had grown fat on.
But there was something strange about the first move being against the temple,
not the Romans.
But perhaps the revolution itself needed some purification first.
We didn't know.
But then everything went quiet.
Whatever was going to happen, it would clearly be later.

The strange thing was nothing much else seemed to happen at all.
For several days all was quiet.
The Temple people were keeping a low profile,
afraid of stirring up trouble,
and Jesus was content to preach,
and to heal people,
and have the occasional argument with the Pharisees.
My friends and I grew impatient.
I saw Judas again and called him over to a group of us.
'Don't worry', he said, 'I think you will see some action tomorrow night.
I've been making arrangements!'
But he would say no more than that.

We saw action all right.
Two days later, Jesus was dead,
crucified by the Romans,
at the instigation of the priests.
It wasn't the way Judas intended, that was for sure,
and later we heard that he had killed himself in remorse.
We went home to think,
and so we missed all the excitement about Jesus being seen alive again,
although we heard about it soon afterwards.
But it did not seem to help the cause of revolution.

CHAPTER THREE • *Christ's Life and Work*

Nothing did.
There were a lot of small provocations went on,
and some bigger insurrections over the next few years,
until in exasperation the Romans besieged Jerusalem,
and destroyed it.
Those few of us who escaped with our lives were very lucky.
Most didn't.

It made me think again about Jesus and His teaching.
We had hated the Romans, who in fairness hadn't treated us too badly.
But what had we got for our efforts?
Only death,
and the loss of the City we loved.
Was there ever any future down that road.
Could we really have ever hoped to win by fighting those well trained troops?
What would have happened if we had done as Jesus said,
If we had tried to love them,
and treat them as brothers.
I don't know.
I knew a few Roman soldiers,
and really they were not much different from us.
There were some rogues, and some villains,
but mostly they were decent men.
Perhaps we could have learned to live together in peace!

I have heard of a group of people who, like us are refugees from Jerusalem,
but these people call themselves 'Christians'.
They are disciples of Jesus,
and they assure everyone who will listen that He is still alive.
I think I will go and find them, and hear what they have to say.
Perhaps they have found the right answers after all,
and if they have, then I would like to share those answers,
and follow in that way.

The Upper Room. A Meditation for Maundy Thursday

I WOULD *ask you to seek to come with me on a meditative and imaginative journey to that upper room, to try to enter as one of those disciples into the atmosphere of that gathering and to hear what our Lord may be saying to each one of us tonight before we ourselves gather round His table here.*

It is a pleasant room,
clean and well furnished,
gleaming with the light of many lamps.
The table is laid with the traditional dishes,
the couches arranged around it,
and we ourselves are bathed and prepared,
for this very special meal.
We gather together,
coming in my twos and threes,
talking, as old friends do, about the trivial events of the day.
But yet, there is a constraint on the conversation;
There are thoughts in our minds we keep to ourselves,
words we do not dare to speak.
We all remember things that Jesus has said to us,
strange and terrible things,
things that we still don't understand,
that we don't really want to hear,
and would rather forget.
But we cannot escape them as they lie in our thoughts
And we are thinking too of the signs of trouble we have seen in the City,
the enmity of the priests,
the scorn and anger of the scribes and pharisees,
and there are rumours of plots and death threats.
Trouble can not be far away.
But not tonight, this special night.
Tonight we are together, and Jesus is with us,

CHAPTER THREE • *Christ's Life and Work*

and we shall speak of hope.
We shall rejoice in the mighty acts of the past
and look forward to the future,
banishing all thoughts of darkness and disaster.

But, for all the lights, there is a darkness hovering in the room.
We can't see it,
but we can feel it.
We cannot banish those dark thoughts with light conversation,
they are part of some evil presence,
hanging, like a thin fog, in the dim corners where the light does not reach.
We sense its presence, yet we know it not.

The meal is ready, and we take our places at the table.
Jesus is our host, and we are pleased and proud to be with Him.
It's time for the foot-washing,
the final cleansing before the ceremonial supper.
It's a task we share in turn.
Whose turn is it tonight?
Is it mine? It may be, I can't remember.
Should I get up and take the bowl?
No! Not tonight, this special night.
I am the guest tonight, not the slave.
Jesus asked me Himself.
Let someone else do it tonight.
I don't want to miss what He is saying.

There is a lull in the conversation.
One of those sudden awkwardness when no-one knows quite what to say.
The darkness in the corners seems to press outwards.
holding back the light from the table.

But what's happening. Jesus is getting up from His place;

He lays His robe aside. Surely He's not going to . . .
He is.
He picks up the bowl and the towel.
He comes forwards and starts to wash our feet.
Jesus Himself, doing the servant's job.
The room is silent.
Just the sound of the water and the scrape and clink of the basin as He moves.
We are too ashamed to even speak.
Until He reaches Peter, last of all,
and Peter can keep silence no longer.
The words that are in the minds of all of us come tumbling out.
'No Lord, You can't wash my feet, it isn't right. I can't let you do that'.
But Jesus, calm as always, answers him.
'Peter, you don't understand now, but you will.
If I do not wash you, you have no part in me'.
For a moment time seems to stand still
in the brief eternal silence.
The whole atmosphere of the room changes.
Peter's voice sounds again, but strangely different.
'Lord, then not my feet only but also my hands and my head'.
We all watch in silence, trying to understand, but we cannot.
Jesus smiles,
'No Peter, there is no need. He who has bathed does not need to wash,
except for his feet.
He is clean all over,
and you are clean, but not all of you'.

There is silence in the room again.
Those last words seem to hang in the air,
sombre and dark, like some half formed threat hanging over us all.
We watch as Jesus puts aside the bowl, takes his robe,
and comes again to his place.
'Do you know what I have done?'

We know.
We are ashamed.
How can we ever forget?
Our Lord and Master has done for us what we ought to have done for Him.
He has taken the slave's task Himself.
Then, His voice comes again. 'I have given you an example. You should do as I have done to you'.

The atmosphere of the room has changed.
Become more serious, more concerned.
There is no more light hearted conversation.
The ritual words are spoken, the responses made.
History comes to life within us,
but that threat of darkness is still there, hovering.
Which of us is unclean?
What is going to happen?
Suddenly there is something unexpected,
quiet words, yet fearful and awesome.
All our dark thoughts come crashing to the forefront of our minds
like a great kaleidoscope of pain and apprehension.
'This is my body which is given for you.
Do this in remembrance of me'.
We eat the bread, passing it from one to another
hardly knowing what we do.
The meal goes on, but we hardly notice in the turmoil of our thoughts.
And the words come again.
'This is the new covenant in my blood'.
Holy Lord God, what does this mean,
What is going to happen?
Jesus speaks again.
His voice cuts through the chaos of our minds,
and the darkness reaches out toward us.
'Behold, the hand of him who betrays me is with me on the table'.

CHAPTER THREE • *Christ's Life and Work*

We look round at each other with questioning and fearful eyes.
Who is it? Is it I?
There is whispering going on but we cannot hear what is said.
It's Peter, and John, and Jesus.
Suddenly Jesus speaks to Judas who gets up from his place.
Perhaps we have forgotten something.
He goes across the room and opens the door.
It's dark outside, very dark.
There must be cloud over the moon.
He goes out and closes the door,
and the feeling of the room changes yet again
as if something evil has followed him out.
There is still a presence,
a dark presence,
the knowledge that something awesome and terrible is waiting to happen,
but somehow its different.
There is a glory in it as well as the fear.
And Jesus is speaking again,
speaking of that glory and of a new commandment,
and of the way in which we must love one another,
as He has loved us.

We cannot remain in that upper room.
The vision fades and the company is gone.
We have shared a poignant moment with them,
but we cannot live for ever in a vision or a dream.
Our life is set in the reality of the present.
But not everything is gone,
there is something we can hold on to,
an even greater reality within the dream,
a reality we can carry within us wherever we go;
a reality we can reach out to and renew within ourselves
day by day and week by week

CHAPTER THREE • *Christ's Life and Work*

a reality that is forever alive
in the sacramental bread and wine of our Lord's table,
and in that living presence which is always with us.

Lord God, grant that our vision of that great reality may never fade
and that we may know the certain assurance of that wonderful presence,
the Holy Spirit,
always at work in our lives,
supporting and guiding us,
leading us always in Your ways of truth,
and love,
and service.
Ever urging us onwards
in the ways You would have us go.
Directing us towards the tasks that You would have us do.
And Lord, we pray that we may fully know
the wonder of Your grace;
the joy of the salvation which Jesus alone can offer;
the knowledge that through His sacrifice we are cleansed from our sins,
even as He cleansed the disciples feet;
and that through that same grace
we may be brought at the end
into the courts of Your glorious Kingdom.
We ask it in the name of Him who has Himself paid the highest of prices for us,
the one in whose name alone we can place our trust,
Jesus Christ, our Saviour and our Redeemer.
Amen.

CHAPTER THREE • *Christ's Life and Work*

The Victory of the Cross

BILLINGSHURST 5TH APRIL 1992

A DISCIPLE *looks back at the Cross and on the journey to Jerusalem which preceded it.*

Those were strange days,
frightening days in many ways,
and as I look back on them now
it seems that we didn't really know Jesus very well at all,
although we thought we did.
Everything had been going so well.
We had been in so many different places
and so much had been done in all of them.
Well, perhaps not quite all.
There had been trouble in Nazareth I remember.
Perhaps it was a foretaste of what was to come.
Or perhaps it was just because the people there knew Jesus too well,
knew Him as a little boy who had grown up with them,
and they could not understand that He was different.
But we had spent much time with Jesus,
learning about the glory of the Kingdom of Heaven,
and about the love of God.
We had watched Him healing people who were sick,
comforting those who were disturbed,
teaching them what was important in life.
He had even sent us out in pairs to continue His work,
and to our surprise we had found we could.
Life was good.
In Jesus we felt we had everything we needed.
Peter spoke for us all when he named Him as the Messiah,
and we expected even greater things to follow.

DEREK JAMES MORRILL • *Meditations*

CHAPTER THREE • *Christ's Life and Work*

And then, suddenly, like the coming of a winter storm,
there was a cold chill,
and everything seemed to start to fall apart.
It was after we had been up north,
on the slopes of Mount Hermon.
Jesus had gone up the mountain with Peter, James and John.
It was a long while before we made sense of what had happened up there.
Jesus didn't say,
and the others were almost incoherent when they came down.
But Jesus was changed in some way
there was a hardness, a determination, about Him which we hadn't really seen before.
Almost the very next day He started speaking to us about His death.
About how His enemies amongst the priesthood would arrange for him to be killed.
It would take place in Jerusalem, He said,
and the answer seemed obvious to us,
Why go there?
There were many others who rejoiced to hear His message.
Many in dire need of His healing power.
Why throw it all away.
But no, He simply said, 'I have go to,
It is what I have come to do'.
And we set off on the long walk back to Jerusalem.
We could not understand.
And when we thought about it a bit more, we were frightened.
If this is what is in store for Him, then what about us?
Were we under threat also?
Thomas was in no doubt about it.
He said openly that we would die with Him.
He was always a pessimist.
But this time it seemed all too likely that he would be proved right.
And we thought, 'What on earth are we doing here?'

Strangely, though we were greatly worried and frightened,

CHAPTER THREE • *Christ's Life and Work*

none of us even thought about deserting Him.
He had always been an outstanding person,
someone with a sort of magnetic attraction about Him.
And we knew Him as someone of deep understanding, and strange powers;
someone close to God.
But now there was something more,
something like an aura of spiritual power about Him,
something so intense that you could almost see it.
More than ever we knew that He was the Messiah, the chosen one,
and yet He was talking about dying.
It didn't make any sort of sense to us, not then at any rate.
Now we can see more clearly.
There was one thing that He said,
that kept turning over in my mind.
He spoke about giving up His life as a ransom for many.
The thought reminded us of buying someone out of slavery,
but most of the people we dealt with were free men.
Except, of course, for our Roman overlords.
But then we expected the Messiah to be able to deal with them.
But how did that get reconciled with death?
We didn't know.
Not then at any rate.

Now we understand better.
You know, of course, of what happened in Jerusalem.
We were totally devastated.
It seemed a total disaster, even worse than we had feared.
And we didn't think we would escape with our lives either.
We had not thought to encounter such viciousness, such evil,
and still less did we think that Jesus could lose such an encounter,
despite what He had said.
Yet it all happened, just as He had foretold,
Even to the last bit which we really had not believed.

DEREK JAMES MORRILL • *Meditations*

CHAPTER THREE • *Christ's Life and Work*

It was Jesus who came out in triumph.
Not the priests, or the Romans.
Death could not hold Him against the power of God's love.
And if death, the last enemy, could not,
then neither could anything else.
And when He came back to us,
and told us that He would be with us always,
even though we would not see Him,
Then we knew that we also were safe in that love.
The priests always told us that the blood of a sacrifice
brought us back to God when we were in the wrong.
But now we know that He was our sacrifice,
A sacrifice which stands for ever,
because God has made it so.
At our last meal together He spoke of it,
spoke of His blood as being the blood of the New Covenant,
And we know that it is true.
For we know that He is alive, and with us,
And that as He dwells in us, so we dwell in Him,
and in Him we are within the Glory of God.
When Jesus was here, we spoke of the kingdom,
because He taught us about it.
Now we will tell the world of the Kingdom,
because we have seen it for ourselves in Him,
and through what He has done we have come to know God
as we have never known Him before.
The Cross was a symbol of shame and suffering,
but to us it has become a symbol of total victory.
And we must share our new knowledge with all men and women. Thanks be to God for His great and steadfast love which He has made known to us in Jesus.
Amen.

CHAPTER FOUR

The Early Church

CHAPTER FOUR • *The Early Church*

The Trinity

BILLINGHURST 6TH JUNE 1993

I SEE *the purpose of a meditation to be to take into the presence of God our understanding of His teaching, so that He can so use our thoughts and words to deepen and enlarge that understanding and draw us closer to Himself. It is not a case of us telling God about things, it is reminding ourselves in His presence how we believe things to be, so that He can guide us into deeper truth as we hold these things in our minds.*

On Trinity Sunday, the Anniversary day of Trinity Church, Billingshurst, how well do we understand this idea of the Trinity? Some have accused us of worshipping not one God, but three. There is an old story that when Christopher Columbus first came in sight of the islands of the West Indies he saw three peaks rising up out of the sea. As he got closer he was able to see that these all belonged to the same island, they were parts of a single entity, and so he named the island Trinidad, which means Trinity, seeing in them a representation of the nature of God Himself.

In our meditation therefore I want to try to dwell for a while on this great paradox of the Trinity, trying to see how the understanding helps us to a greater knowledge of God and fellowship with Him.

O Lord our God, You are our God, and we would be Your people,
But when we turn to You we are often filled with questions.
How are we to understand You?
How should we come to You and what do You require of us?
We know of You as the Creator of the Universe, the giver of life;
Master and Lord of all that is,
from things too small for us to see,
to worlds and stars whose size and distance we cannot comprehend.
And as Creator of all this vastness, You too are beyond our comprehension,
Master and Lord of things infinitely great and infinitely small
You are greater than all these things.
We can see the reflection of Your glory all around us in Your creation,
but Yourself we cannot see.
And beside Your greatness we are small and fearful creatures.
We know Your power and might, and we fear Your judgement upon our lives.

We hear Your call to obedience, but we know our failings and inability.
We are people of unclean lips and we tremble as we await Your cleansing.

O Lord our God, how are we to know You better?
How may we see Your face in all the light of Glory?
You come to us in Jesus, sharing in our humanity,
to show us what You are truly like.
In Him we see Your glory, shrunk down to human size,
He is a man as we are men and women, yet You are present in Him.
And, through Him, You speak to us of Yourself.
Through Him we can see Creation itself as an act of love,
We can see ourselves as children, begotten of a loving Father.
A Father who calls His children to His side,
Not in judgement, but in love,
Seeking to complete and perfect His creation in a relationship of love.

But Jesus is more than just an image of the Father to us.
We rejoice that we can know that anyone who has seen jesus has seen the Father,
But there is more to see and understand there.
For in Jesus we can also see ourselves,
Not in the fragility and failure of our earthly image,
but as we might be;
as You would have us be.
In Him we can see the perfection of the relationship to which You call us.
A relationship of perfect trust, perfect obedience;
A relationship of love.
And we see too Your assurance that that perfect relationship is eternal and unbreakable.
That Your love is stronger than the power of sin;
Stronger than death itself.

But when we see ourselves in Him,
we also see ourselves in the light of Your Glory,
And we are ashamed, for in that light

we see ourselves as we truly are.
And we know as we look how far we fall short of that perfect image.
We know our own inability to put things right,
And we know that we cannot do any good thing except through Your goodness and grace.
But in Him we see too Your helping hand,
stretched out towards us,
And we hear Your voice saying, 'Come! Poor as you are'.
'Put your trust in me'.
'Take my hand and let me make you into the perfect creation that I intended from the beginning'.

Yet still, Lord God, we ask,
How are we to know You better?
How should we see Your face in the light of Your glory?
How are we to know Your presence in the world today?
You come to us today through Your Holy Spirit,
And in that Spirit You would dwell within us
present with us even as You were incarnate in Jesus,
and only the poverty of our faith can stand between us.
Only our denial can refuse You entry.
But we can open ourselves to You,
we can know Your presence with us.
We can sometimes hear Your voice giving us guidance and instruction.
We can know Your reassurance of Your love, the peace of Your presence,
in times of trouble and distress.
We can hear the challenge of Your voice when there are tasks to do.
It is the very Spirit of truth,
And we can know that truth for in Jesus You have shared in every part of our lives.
The presence which You bring to us is the God who made us,
Who gave us life,
and He is also the God who partook of the life of that creation.
You dwell in us not just as some distant entity,
but as part of our very selves as well.

O Lord our God, Creator, Judge, and loving Father,
We adore You.
O Lord our God, incarnate in jesus Christ the Son,
living in loving obedience, dying for our sins,
and conquering even death itself to show us Your love,
We adore You.
O Lord our God, dwelling within each one of Your people as the Holy Spirit,
bringing to us knowledge and understanding of You and of ourselves,
We adore You.
Grant, we pray, an ever deepening knowledge of Your presence
and implant within us an ever increasing faith,
that we may perfectly trust You,
and live with You in loving obedience,
even as Jesus showed us,
for we ask it in His name.
Amen.

Peter Looks Back on the Transfiguration

IT WAS something quite unforgettable,
a day above all days, or almost all days.
There have been other, greater, days since,
Passover, with its cross and the shattering loneliness,
and the day we found Jesus was still alive;
Pentecost, when the Spirit fell upon us.
But that was the day when we began to understand
dimly, at least,
who Jesus really was
and something of what it meant to be God's anointed one.

We thought that we knew, of course.
Only the week before
up north, near Caesarea Philippi,
He had asked us, Who do you think I am?
And in that moment I knew the truth,
though I didn't know what the truth was.
'You are the Christ!' I said.
The words seemed to come without any conscious intent on my part.
It was knowledge coming to me from God Himself.
Jesus told me so, and I believe Him.
But I thought I knew what the Christ was to be;
but then He started speaking about rejection and death.
His death.
And I could not bear it.
'Surely not this Lord', I said,
'Surely the Christ must be welcomed, not rejected!
Will you not lead us to freedom, to power?'
But that was not the voice of God, that was Satan speaking,
and He would have none of it, He would not even speak about it

CHAPTER FOUR • *The Early Church*

He sent me aside, and I did not understand.

I still did not understand when He called James and John, and myself.
'Come with me!' he said, 'We will go up the mountain'.
It was early in the morning,
Still dark,
and the mist was blowing in patches.
We were tired,
there had been little sleep that week,
for we were all disturbed, and worried.
There was darkness within as well as round about.
And as we climbed there was a feeling of growing apprehension.
Something was going to happen,
but what was it!
A feeling of awesome fear weighed upon us.
The path was steep but that feeling weighed upon us more than the steepness
How much further can we go?
Then He spoke,
'We shall wait here a while'.
It was almost dawn
The sky was brightening in the east,
but in our weariness we slumped to the ground.
Perhaps we dozed in the quietness.
It was not a time for talking,
or a place.
It felt as though the barrier which divided us from another world
was wearing very thin.
If we spoke, would someone else hear as well?
Suddenly we were wide awake
and scared stiff.
The place was flooded with light.
It wasn't the dawn; this was no sunlight
It streamed from Jesus himself,

DEREK JAMES MORRILL • *Meditations*

CHAPTER FOUR • *The Early Church*

from His face,
from His clothes.
And there were others with Him.
Moses.
Elijah.
They had not spoken any words that we could hear,
but we knew them.
Knowledge came to us; we just knew.
We could not bear to stay near,
yet even more we could not bear to run away.
We could not stand the presence,
but we wanted that presence to stay for ever.
'Should we make three shelters?' I asked,
but it was foolishness, and I knew it.
Then a cloud swept down,
not the patchy mist of the mountain
but a real cloud;
more than a real cloud;
We fell on our faces.
A great voice spoke from the cloud.
We did not need to ask whose voice it was.
When God speaks, no-one need be in any doubt.
'This is my beloved son, with whom I am well pleased,
Listen to Him'.
We buried our faces in the ground
we dare not look up.
Time passed.
Suddenly Jesus touched us and spoke to us,
and we looked up.
The great light, the crowd, the figures, were all gone.
There was just Jesus,
with the light of the rising sun shining on Him.
He looked just the same, and yet there was a difference.

He was always confident, always strong,
but now He seemed stronger,
invincible,
and sure of Himself.
He told us that what we had seen belonged to the future
and we must not speak of it until that future time came,
the time when He should have risen from the dead.
We had seen a foretaste of the glory that was to come,
and henceforth we should have no doubts.
We did, of course.
We still didn't really understand,
and there were dreadful days ahead.
But now, we do understand
We saw the Glory of God on that day
Glory resting upon Jesus Himself;
Glory that will be seen again on earth
on that day when He shall come again.
We have seen His victory on earth;
How shall we doubt any more?

Father, as we hear the experience of Peter
coming through to us from the pages of Your word,
May we too doubt no more, but believe.
Keep the vision of Your Glory always before us
that we may be strong in our faith
and loyal in our service
for Jesus' sake.
Amen.

CHAPTER FOUR • *The Early Church*

Ananias Looks Back

BILLINGSHURST 5TH AUGUST 1990
PULBOROUGH 27TH JANUARY 1991

SO PAUL'S work is done, and He has given His life for Christ.
A staunch witness to the end, and not likely to bow to the Emperor's will.
He was not a man whose mind was easy to change,
once he had decided what was right;
not a man for giving up once he had set himself to a task.
And yet, I still remember how God changed his mind for him once,
stopped him in his tracks and set him on a new road,
the road of service to Christ.
I don't suppose there has ever been any greater change in a man than that.
It would have been about 30 years ago now,
yet I remember it as well as if it had been yesterday.
It had been a long hot summer in Damascus.
Everything was dried up, the winter rains had not yet come.
We received news of our fellow christians in Jerusalem.
More than news alone, there were refugees also,
friends who had been forced to run away to escape arrest.
And there was one man's name on most of their lips,
the name of Saul, a man of Tarsus originally,
a pharisee with a deep and abiding hatred for those who followed the Way;
the way of service to Jesus Christ.
It seemed that he had some sort of authority from the Sanhedrin,
authority to arrest any practising christians and throw them in prison.
The prisons were full in Jerusalem.
We knew of many people who had been flogged to make them turn away from Christ.
Some had died; many families broken up.
And then there was word that this terrible man was coming here, to Damascus.
We all feared the trouble he would bring.
Some of the more fearful among us were literally terrified.

CHAPTER FOUR • *The Early Church*

And then it was rumoured that he had already come,
that he was here in the city.
He had been seen with a large band of guards.
Clearly the axe was about to fall,
but when? And where?
The fellowship was full of rumours,
but hard facts were difficult to come by,
and that made it all the more fearsome.
There's nothing worse than uncertainty.

For two or three days this went on, this waiting for something to happen.
And then, that night, I couldn't sleep for worrying, and for the heat.
But, as I dozed uncertainly I heard a voice.
It called my name; 'Ananias, Ananias'.
There was no-one else in the house that night,
my wife was away on a visit and I was alone.
I could not make out who was calling me.
But the call came again. 'Ananias'.
Suddenly I realised what was happening.
Surely it was the Lord calling me.
So I answered Him, 'Yes Lord, I am here'.
And the voice spoke again.
That was a fearsome enough thing of itself, to hear the voice of the risen Christ,
But the words that He spoke seemed to freeze the blood in my veins.
'In the house of Judas, in the street called Straight,
go and enquire and you will find Saul of Tarsus'.
Saul of Tarsus! the man we all feared and hated,
and less than a Sabbath's day journey away.
I didn't want to do any enquiring or finding.
'Lord', I said, 'Surely you know what sort of man this is,
how much harm he is doing to Your people.
And You are asking me to go and find him.
I would much rather go the other way; fast'.

CHAPTER FOUR • *The Early Church*

But the voice went on, 'No Ananias, that won't do.
I have shown myself to him and spoken with him.
Now he is blind, and he has been praying and fasting for three days.
He has seen a vision of Ananias coming to lay hands on him
that he might receive his sight'.
And the voice went on,
'You must go to him, because I have chosen him to do great work for me amongst the Gentiles.
It won't be easy for him either, he will suffer much in my service.
But you must be the one to go to him now'.

I resisted the thought. How could I do a thing like that.
Could the Lord really want me to put my neck into the noose like this?
But I heard no different message,
just that quiet voice saying 'Go!'
and I knew that I would have to go.
If my love for Jesus was real, how could I ignore His call?
I got up and dressed, for it was then coming light.
I couldn't eat any breakfast, I was still too frightened,
but I knew what I had to do.
I went out and walked straight to the place.
There was no trouble finding it,
and straightaway they showed me to a small upper room.
Saul of Tarsus lay on a bed, I recognised him from his description.
I went over to him.
It was obvious he could not see. His eyes were crusted over.
'I am Ananias', I said.
'The Lord has sent me to restore your sight,
that you may be filled with the new light of the Holy Spirit'.
I had been shaking with fear when I went into the room,
but then, as I laid my hands on his head, there was a great sense of peace,
and a feeling of power and heat, the power of the Holy Spirit.
The great crusts fell away from his eyes, and they opened, and he sat up.

'I have been a fool', he said,
'and worse than that I have sought to defy the Holy one of God.
But now I know that He has forgiven me and called me to serve.
From now on I will do nothing but His will'.
We went out together, to the nearest pool of water,
There I baptised him, and we knelt together in prayer,
giving thanks to God for all His wondrous deeds.
Then we returned home, to my home, and I prepared food for us both.
For several days we talked together, mostly about Jesus, but about his followers also.
Then he started to speak in the Synagogues.
People were amazed, for all knew what he had been doing and saying before
and few people could believe the change was real.
But I knew. I had been there, the chosen agent through whom it all happened.
It was real enough.
The power which had brought it about had flowed for a moment through my hands.
And that alone is something I shall never forget.

Saul had to run away from Damascus soon after.
Many of the Jews could not stand the change in him and they plotted to kill him.
He had to go over the wall by night to escape.
We never met again, but I have always sought news of him,
and of the great work he has done.
It seems strange that it all had to begin through me,
But then, who can fathom the ways of God,
and how He chooses to use us in His service.

CHAPTER FOUR • *The Early Church*

Onesimus: Bishop of Ephesus

BILLINGHURST 1ST MARCH 1992

IT'S STRANGE somehow, to look back over a lifetime
and to think about the meaning of what has happened.
How even the bad things often turn out to be good in the end.
My earliest memories are of the life of a slave,
and that was certainly not good,
even though Philemon, my master, was a good and kindly man.
But if I hadn't been a slave
I might never have met Paul,
and certainly would never have become a Bishop.
It reminds me of the story of Joseph in a way,
for if Joseph's brothers hadn't sold him as a slave,
all his family might well have died of starvation,
unless God had found out some other way to save them.

I don't think I was very much use as a slave.
My name, you know, means useful.
But I never gave a proper return for my master's goodness to me.
There was too much resentment within me.
I hated being a slave.
There's something evil about being in bondage to another man
and I wanted freedom more than anything else.
My opportunity came when a man named Paul came to visit.
I didn't hear much of what he said for my duties mostly kept me outside,
but what he had to say had a profound effect upon the household.
My master's life seemed to be changed
and for a while after he left, the household was disorganised.
and I took my chance to escape,
taking some food and a little money to keep me alive.
I ran as fast as I could for a bit to get away from people who might know me

CHAPTER FOUR • *The Early Church*

but afterwards I travelled more slowly
so as not to draw attention to myself.
Eventually I reached Ephesus where I found work and lodgings,
and in that crowded city I felt quite safe from detection.
I was free at last, I thought.
Then, one day, quite a while later, someone told me about a man named Paul.
And when he described him I realised I had seen him before.
It was the same man who had visited my master.
He had been preaching in the synagogue but had been expelled.
It seemed that his fellow Jews did not like what he had to say.
But some friends had hired the hall of Tyrannus for him,
and every day he was teaching there,
and quite large crowds came into hear him.
I was intrigued.
I knew the effect he had had upon my master,
and I wanted to know more.
I didn't think he had seen enough of me in Colossae to recognise me again.
So I went and listened to him.
For the first time I heard the Good News of the Gospel,
about Jesus who died for our sins,
and rose again to lead us into eternal life.
I didn't understand it all at first,
I went back several times to hear more.
And as I listened it came upon me that this was important to me.
This new understanding, this living presence of which Paul spoke
was something I had to have.
So one day I went to Paul after he had finished speaking to the people
and asked to know more,
and to be baptised into this new faith.
We talked together, many times,
and Paul was teaching me all the time,
teaching me how to know the presence of the living God.
We became so close that I could not bear to be parted from him.

CHAPTER FOUR • *The Early Church*

He became like a father to me,
and when the authorities threw him into prison
because of some agitation about his preaching,
I went along with him as his servant and one of his companions.
But our relationship was not entirely perfect.
Despite our closeness there remained some sort of barrier between us,
And both of us were aware of it at times.
Then one day Paul questioned me about it,
and I admitted that I was not a freeman, but was a runaway slave,
with a slave's price on my head.

Paul considered this for a while,
then he spoke to me.
'You can't escape from bondage just by running away', he said.
'We have to face up to this situation and sort it out properly.
I know Philemon and I think we can set things right
but I don't want to lose you.
You have become truly useful to me,
and I believe God has a calling for you to follow'.
And then he told me that I should have to go back,
but that he would send someone with me
another of his friends from those parts,
a man named Tychicus who had been with us in Ephesus for some time.
Tychicus would carry a letter from Paul to Philemon.
This didn't sound a very good idea.
I didn't think Philemon would have me killed,
although he could have done according to the law.
But I could expect a sound beating at least.
But Paul said not to worry,
he was sure everything would be all right,
and eventually he convinced me that this was the right thing to do.

So the two of us went back to Colossae,

CHAPTER FOUR • *The Early Church*

to the house of Philemon.
He looked very stern when he saw me,
but Tychicus delivered the letter
and Philemon took time to read it.
As he read, I saw his face soften.
'Do you know what Paul is asking for you?' he asked.
'No'. I replied, 'I have not read the letter'.
'He is asking me, in a round-about way,
to let you go back to him as a free man,
and he will pay your debts.
Do you think that is reasonable?'
My spirits sank.
Of course it wasn't reasonable.
And Paul could not afford to pay in any case.
But Philemon went on.
'I owe Paul a great deal', he said,
'And if I judge matters rightly, you also owe him a similar debt.
Has he not given to you also the knowledge of Jesus Christ
and of his salvation?'
'Oh yes!' I replied, 'Without that I would never have dared come back'.
'Well', said Philemon, 'For Paul's sake, but most of all for Jesus' sake,
I will agree to his request.
Your debt is cancelled, and you can return to him'.
I fell on my knees before him,
too overcome to be able to talk sensibly,
to thank him properly.
But he didn't want my thanks.
Not like that anyway.
'Stand up', he said,
'You are a slave no longer in worldly terms,
But I sense that Jesus is calling you to much greater service,
and much harder work than I would set you to.
Go now. Learn your calling, and serve Him'.

CHAPTER FOUR • *The Early Church*

And I have done just that.
A few days later we returned to Paul in Ephesus.
I remained with him until he was released and left the town,
and then continued to serve the church he had founded
as well as I could.
I have done many jobs and tackled many different tasks
and eventually they made me Bishop,
a position I have filled for many years now.
But I have never forgotten Paul who taught me so much.
And the first thing I did as Bishop
was to make a collection of as many of his letters as could be found.
Some were in fragments, some lost completely.
But I gathered them together and copied them,
and published them for others to read.
And, to my great joy, at Colossae
I found the letter to Philemon that started it all.
Then for the first time I could read it properly,
and I realised what a masterly piece of writing it was.
I am sure that the Lord was with Paul when he wrote it,
And for that matter, with Philemon when he read it,
And that everything has, in the end, worked out the way He wanted.
Thanks be to God who brings all things into His good purposes.

The Christian Scribe

THE *book of Acts tells us that included amongst the many people who accepted Jesus as Lord after the Resurrection were a considerable number of the Priests of the day. I think that we can take this as an indication that a wide cross section of the people became believers, including some of the scribes and pharisees. It would probably be amongst people of this sort of background that all the controversy over Jewish Law and circumcision grew up later. But converts in Jerusalem immediately after the crucifixion were probably large people who had heard Jesus speak before His death, and we cannot imagine that His words did not have their influence on the later decision. I want tonight to consider one such person, who we will imagine as being one of the scribes among the party who were sent to test Jesus with difficult questions, and to think what his thoughts and reactions might be as he looks back at his experience. Perhaps his testimony would go something like this.*

My name is Joiadah and I was trained as a scribe, but now I am a Christian.
I spend my time nowadays writing about Jesus.
I actually became a Christian six weeks after Pentecost,
or at least, that was when I was baptised.
I had heard Peter and some of the other disciples speaking of jesus
and of the way in which He had died,
and had come back to them.
They spoke of the way in which Jesus had called them,
and in turn, they were calling on others.
I had felt as though I was being pulled in several ways at once,
but, when Peter spoke, I felt sure that he was right.
Jesus was truly the one to follow.
But that wasn't where it all started for me.
That had been some time before, when Jesus entered Jerusalem.
He had come down the Mount of Olives riding on a donkey,
and people were shouting and cheering, and calling Him the Messiah,
the King who came in the name of the Lord.
I remember that on that day we were in a committee meeting,
trying to settle a point of the law which someone had brought to us.

CHAPTER FOUR • *The Early Church*

Messengers came in to tell us what was happening.
I was a junior member of that meeting and so I kept quiet
but my seniors had plenty to say, mostly neither polite nor friendly I remember.
Not that the messengers were all that necessary, for we were near the temple
and we could hear and see for ourselves.
But one messenger was different, he came from Annas, the old high priest,
and he was exceedingly upset.
His traders had been thrown out of the temple
and in the riot a good deal of money went mysteriously astray.
Something had to be done, we were told, but how?
It was decided to try to trap Jesus into some admission
which could be used against Him.
So a group of us went to Him in the Temple a few days later and challenged Him.
'Why do you do these things? Where does your authority come from?' we asked.
But He threw the question straight back at us.
'First tell me whether the baptism of John was from men, or from God', He said.
There was a murmur from the crowd who were gathered round us
and we had a whispered discussion amongst ourselves.
'We must be careful here. If we say from God, we've lost our case.
Everyone knows that John revered Jesus.
But that mob over there have stones in their hands
and they think John was a prophet of God'.
So our leader wouldn't answer.
He said we didn't know.
And of course, Jesus refused to answer us,
just as we might have expected.

We were just about to turn away and leave when Jesus started to tell a story.
A story about a vineyard.
A man planted it, put a wall round it and built a tower in it,
fitted it out with all its equipment and let it out to tenants.
So far it was a familiar story, a common occurrence,
but already we scribes had recognised its significance.

CHAPTER FOUR • *The Early Church*

It came from the book of the prophet Isaiah.
And in that story, the vineyard was God's vineyard,
It was Israel and Judah.
This was a story about the Jewish people.
And when He went on to speak bout the tenants, He looked straight at us,
and the thought came to me, 'If Israel is the vineyard,
then we who tend and guide Israel must be the tenants.
So what's he going to say about us?
Then Jesus went on to talk about the harvest time.
The Landlord sent servants to collect the rent.
But the tenants wouldn't pay.
Instead they roughed the servants up and sent them away empty handed.
Some they wounded.
It happened like that sometimes.
With a landlord far away the tenants get arrogant
and want to keep it all for themselves.
But then I remembered the story setting.
These messengers were intended to be God's servants,
and that must mean the prophets,
and I thought back about how ill some of them had been received.
And we were being blamed for that!
Suddenly I felt very angry. We always did our best to keep Israel pure.
Was this all the thanks we got?
But the story went on.
The Landlord's beloved son was sent.
But He was not respected either.
The tenants rather saw their chance to claim the inheritance for themselves
by doing away with Him.
I didn't altogether understand this at first,
but then I remembered what someone had told me
about Jesus baptism two or three years earlier.
It was said that there had been a voice from heaven saying,
'This is my beloved Son, in whom I am well pleased'.

CHAPTER FOUR • *The Early Church*

I hadn't thought much about it at the time,
I put it all down to imagination,
But now it came back to me, quite strongly.
Was Jesus claiming to be the Son of God,
and also foretelling His death?
Not that that was unlikely, the way things were going.
But were we to be blamed for that?
I didn't know. We were all a bit confused, as well as angry.
But the story wasn't finished.
This landlord was powerful.
He would come with many men and destroy the tenants,
and give the vineyard to better men.
Again, that seemed quite normal,
a bit illegal perhaps, but not uncommon.
And then again I thought of the story context.
This landlord was God! and I was one of the tenants!
Would God destroy me?
I didn't think I deserved it.
And then Jesus looked straight at us as He said,
'Scripture says that the stone which the builders rejected
this has become the head of the corner.
Everyone who falls on that stone will be shattered,
but if it falls on anyone it will wipe them out
as the wind blows the chaff away'.
I knew the scripture of course, but the way He applied it was new.
I wasn't sure it was right, but I couldn't stop thinking about it.
Or about the whole story.
Were we really such guilty men?
Was such death and punishment really possible?

And then we heard about the plans to destroy Jesus.
I didn't feel I wanted to be involved,
but I went along with the others.

Jesus was arrested:
one of his disciplines betrayed Him to us for a small sum.
Within a few hours He was dead,
and I, and one or two friends who had been thinking on similar lines,
thought about that story,
and about the punishment that would surely come if He was right.
And then came the news that He had been seen alive again.
We found that hard to believe, but strangely the authorities couldn't produce the body.
All they could do was cook up a tale that the body had been stolen.
But everyone knew that it had been guarded, just to prevent such a thing.
Then we heard Peter and the others speaking.
They were brutally direct.
'Yes, He was the Son of God, the promised Messiah.
And you killed Him.
Or at least you arranged it or went along with it,
and that's just as bad.
But God has reversed what you have done
and in Jesus name we offer you the chance to repent,
to start again.
It's God promise'.
I thought about it for some time,
and I thought about how Jesus had looked at me while He told that story.
And I knew I couldn't live with my old life,
and so I was baptised.
I asked to be forgiven, and I was.
It's not just words, I know God has forgiven me,
Just as I know that Jesus is alive and with us still.
God's love is stronger than any earthly story,
stronger than we can imagine.
I cannot comprehend it, but I know it now for myself.
It is knowledge which has changed my life.
It can change everyone else's life too.
Thanks be to God for all His steadfast love.

CHAPTER FIVE

God with Us

CHAPTER FIVE • *God with Us*

1st Meditation: the Law of Love

FATHER, in Jesus Christ You have spoken to us,
spoken the decisive word,
made plain Your new covenant of love.
'He who has seen me has seen the Father,'
Those were Jesus words.
And we do see Him,
through the pages of scripture,
through our sharing in the Sacrament,
through our own experience of His presence.
But we do not see clearly,
although we sometimes think that we do.
We know this, for we know we do not all see the same,
Yet You are one.
You are the eternal, unchanging one.
And if we could see You clearly, we would know.
and the arguments would be over,
but they are not.
Lord, help us all to see you more clearly,
and help us to know where our vision is still clouded and imperfect.
Help us to open our hearts to You,
that You might inscribe Your law and image there.
Give us such a vision of yourself
and of our calling,
that we might cease to worry about the imperfections
and simply come to You,
and follow you,
as one single fellowship of brothers and sisters in Christ,
sharing with each other the vision that You grant us,
each helping to bring closer that glorious day
when we shall no longer need to share and discuss these things,

for each of us will know You
in the fullness and wonder of Your Glory,
and all people shall worship You together,
Blending their different voices into one song.
Lord, in Your mercy, hear our prayers.

2ND MEDITATION: TESTING BY FIRE

LORD, as we praise You and Bless Your Holy Name,
strengthen our faith,
Help our understanding,
Clear away our errors and our misinterpretations,
Renew within us that living hope
and give us a new vision of our imperishable inheritance.
And in the strength of that renewed faith,
help us to be able to share our vision with other Christians,
without concern and worry that their vision may be different.
Help all of us to hear when others tell us we are wrong,
not with anger at their arrogance,
but knowing that You may be speaking to us through their words,
or perhaps speaking to them through us!
Help us to know that the inheritance which You give to us
is truly our inheritance,
and truly theirs as well.
Lord, we do not like to be told, quite bluntly,
'You are wrong.'
But sometimes we know that we are.
Sometimes too, we know that it can be a destructive word,
intended to weaken us
and force us into new ways.
ways not of our choosing, or of Yours.
But sometimes too it can be Your word,

seeking to open our minds and our eyes,
allowing new truth to enter.
Even when we're not wrong
We may not be wholly right either.
Help us to stand up for our faith
and to argue for what we believe.
For we believe that faith comes from You.
But help us also that we may argue with eyes and ears open
listening for the truth in other words,
seeing the vision that other eyes may see
that greater truth may emerge from the testing,
that faith itself may not be weakened,
but rather that it should be strengthened
With new thoughts, new understanding,
and a wider grasp of Your truth,
so that more and more voices may combine in Your praise.
May this work continue and grow,
until the whole world can join with the angelic choir
to give glory to Your name throughout the earth.
Lord, in Your mercy, hear our prayer.

3RD MEDITATION: THE GLORY OF GOD

FATHER, each of us has within ourselves
a little castle of privacy which we guard jealously.
For within that castle we are King.
And all that we think and do within is, we believe, our business,
and so very important in our eyes.
And we believe that we can control what comes in and what goes out.
Even sometimes we may believe that we can control You.
Or at least that we can define You
and understand the fullness of Your word for us.

Father, forgive our arrogance and stupidity.
Break down the walls of our selfish castles
and let Your Glory shine within.
Show us the true vision of Your greatness,
that we may better understand our own insignificance.
Help us to get our sense of proportion right,
that we may be able to assess the true importance
of our little concerns
against the immensity of Your power, and Your love.
For You stand above us as the heavens spread over the earth,
and we are as the blades of grass in the field.
And yet we know that You call each one of us,
and know us,
and we rejoice in wonder at that mighty word.

We need this same vision for our churches, Father.
We have each striven to build our own ivory tower,
seeking to lift ourselves to Your presence,
fencing ourselves off with a wall of private understanding
so that those who do not share it with us may not come in.
Help us to see how useless this activity is.
For the greatest of our towers cannot bring us to Your presence
unless You bring that presence to us.
Help us to know that whatever vision we may have of Your glory,
we only have it as You have given it to us.
Make us to know that such visions are not given for one alone,
or even for one group alone,
but are to be shared with all Your people,
even as they share their vision with us.
Help us to see ourselves as You see us, Father
Arguing over authority on earth
while You hold the Sun and Moon in the palm of Your hand.
Solemnly debating the nature of Your real presence

CHAPTER FIVE • *God with Us*

even while we are surrounded and encompassed by Your steadfast love.
Worrying about words and forms,
and deaf to the sound of the heavenly host singing Your praise.
Father, lift us high above the barriers of trivia we have erected
and fill us with the joy of life together in Your love.
Lord, in Your mercy, hear our prayers.

4TH MEDITATION: THE TRUE VINE

FATHER, You are the source of all life,
and from You alone comes the nourishment which can maintain it.
You sent the gift of Jesus into the world
that through Him the world might be reconciled to You;
that through Him we might restore those life giving ties
through which alone we can live.
He is the connection between us and You,
His body the strength and support which holds us up,
His blood the source of our renewal, our salvation to life eternal.
He is one with You, and one with us,
and we join our voices with the whole creation crying,
'To Him who sits upon the throne, and to the Lamb,
be blessing and honour and glory and might,
for ever and ever. Amen.'
Lord, we acknowledge that we are one in Christ,
that You have not called us with different voices,
but with one voice,
one eternal Word.
And we rejoice in that acknowledgement,
remembering how much more real it has become in recent years.
And yet we do not know how to make it fully real.
We know that we are but separate branches on the one vine,
yet we do not always feel close together,

and sometimes we know we are far apart still.
Help us all to know, with a great and true certainty,
that the only way we can separate ourselves from each other,
is to separate ourselves from You.
And that is the separation of death.
Help us all to trace the source of our life back to the trunk,
to Jesus,
and through Him to You.
Help us to start our thinking and our understanding afresh,
starting from our unity in Him,
and holding firmly to that unity
as we trace the pattern of branches once again,
that the great vine of life may become once again
the fruitful tree that You would have it be.
Lord, you have promised through Your apostle Paul,
that if we hold fast to Your love,
that love which You bring to us in Jesus,
nothing in heaven or on earth will be able to separate us from You.
This must mean, Father,
that nothing can separate us from each other either.
So help us all, Father, to take such a fresh hold on Your love,
that this promise may be fulfilled in the life of our churches.
That the whole world may see Your glory.
And, we pray, that we may share in the joy of that fulfilment also.
Lord, in Your mercy, hear our prayer.

Chapter Five • *God with Us*

Gethsemane, a Look Back in Time

PETWORTH 16TH APRIL 1992

IT WAS on a Thursday evening in Jerusalem.
A group of us met in St Mark's church,
a small place, but one where Jesus may have met with His disciples,
on that Thursday so many years ago.
There is a picture on the wall, clearly very old,
of a mother with a baby.
A picture of Mary with Jesus.
Many believe it to be from the hand of St Luke himself.
The language here is Old Syriac.
As close as one can get to the Amaraic which Jesus spoke,
And so we listen to His words in the very tones He used,
as He spoke of His body, and His blood.
And then, in silence, we think of Him
in that special place.

And we continue in silence as we leave,
walking along narrow streets and alleys,
Past the Temple wall to the Dung gate,
and out onto the roadway down the Kidron valley.
It is a modern thing, this road,
scraped out of the side of the steep valley.
Jesus path would have been steeper
and lower down.
To the right there is the sheer drop down to the valley floor,
With Absalom's tomb in the shadows below,
a landmark He would have known.
To our left, towering up above us in a sudden burst of moonlight
The wall, and the pinnacle of the Temple.
And, in the silence and the shadowed light

CHAPTER FIVE • *God with Us*

We are transported back to those times,
and we are with the disciples,
following our Lord out of Jerusalem.
Knowing that something terrible was happening,
but not knowing what it would turn out to be.
And Jesus, too, looks up to that towering height beside us.
He hesitates, and an expression of pain crosses His face,
and He looks away again,
and resumes his steady, purposeful walk down the valley.
What grim thought has come to Him there?
We know not,
But the pain on His face adds to our burden of foreboding,
and the sound of our footsteps on the stony path
echo in the silence of the valley.

Across the valley bottom and a little way up the opposite slope
we come to the garden entrance.
The gate is open and we go in,
picking our way through the shadows of the Olive trees,
Our feet crunching on the stones.
Jesus and three of his friends go apart a little way.
We sit on the stones in the fitful moonlight
and all is quiet, save only for the rustle of the olive leaves
stirred by the gentle breeze.
One by one, the disciples fall asleep,
weary after a long day,
and overcome with many almost unbearable thoughts.
And then we heard Jesus voice,
an agonizing plea that seems to freeze the blood in our veins,
'Father, all things are possible to Thee, remove this cup from me;
yet not what I will, but what Thou wilt'.
What dreadful thing is this?
And His words about death and sacrifice arise again before us

CHAPTER FIVE • *God with Us*

with dreadful finality.
And suddenly we know
with a terrible certainty,
just what the thought was that had assailed Him on that valley road.
Satan himself,
offering the easy way,
reminding Him of that desert experience three years ago.
'Throw yourself down from that pinnacle, and all the world will follow you'
'Thou shalt not put the Lord Your God to the test!'
'Father, Thy will be done'.
The sheer violence of that conflict appals and terrifies us
Jesus has a choice.
But instinctively we know that the choice is wrong.
It's not God's choice, but Satan's.
And will not God strengthen Him to make the right choice?
Life depends upon it!

Suddenly the silence is broken.
There is a noise of steel on steel,
a crunching of booted feet on the stones,
lights between the trees.
A voice comes softly,
'Come this way, this is where He usually comes to pray'
And for a while, all is confusion.
And then, above the noise, Jesus voice, strong and commanding?
'Do you think I cannot appeal to my Father,
and He will at once send me more than twelve legions of angels!
But let the scriptures be fulfilled'.
And the horror of the choice crowds in on us again.
It was a real choice,
Jesus' choice.
And God would have honoured it either way.
He could have escaped with God's power at His call,

CHAPTER FIVE • *God with Us*

and no-one could have stopped Him.
But in love, He said,
'Thy will be done, however bitter the cup'.

There is silence all around us.
The moon comes from behind a cloud,
and the garden is empty,
we have only the olives for company,
yet the memories are alive
and will remain.
We have seen real love in action,
sacrificial love,
love beyond our comprehension.
And we look forward to Easter,
to the triumph of that love,
and the gift of salvation that it brings.
But in Gethsemane we have seen
something of the pain and the cost of that salvation.
We have seen Jesus,
battling with the power of evil,
a struggle that would continue on the cross
and beyond.
A struggle undertaken in faith for us,
a conflict which brings us a victory we can never deserve.

Lord, keep us aware of the cost of our redemption,
of the power of Love which alone could pay that cost,
Take us in our unworthiness and cleanse us;
mould us into the likeness You would have us bear,
that we might become in the strength of Your love,
disciples who are worthy of the sacrifice which has been made for us.
For we ask it in Jesus name.
Amen.

CHAPTER FIVE • *God with Us*

'Acceptable Worship'

BILLINGSHURST 2ND FEBRUARY 1992

THIS IS Your house today, Lord,
The place where we gather as Your people,
Hoping to find You,
Bringing our offering of worship and praise.
Seeking Your acceptance;
Seeking the assurance of Your love,
as men and women have sought throughout all generations.
We know that You can be worshipped in many ways,
Yet Scripture tells us that we must offer acceptable worship,
and we need to understand what this means
and sometimes the words seem contradictory
Sometimes they have been interpreted in different ways
and perhaps we have missed the point
and need to look again.

In ancient times there was but one Temple.
The place where You had placed Your name
and many worshipped You there.
It was a place of blood and smoke
with sacrifices and burnt offerings;
a place which seems very strange to us today.
But You were there,
and what was done was according to Your instruction.
In that place You revealed Yourself to the prophet Isaiah,
and in that place You spoke to many,
and they heard Your words and did Your will.
Yet there came a time when You would not hear Your people's song;
a time when You would not look at their feasts,
and their sacrifice was not acceptable in Your sight.

The words were the same,
The songs had not changed
The people put their trust in You as they had before,
Yet to no avail.
Your name was withdrawn,
Your House was destroyed,
and people worshipped You elsewhere.
Your prophets tell us that Your people had failed You,
that they did not keep Your commandments,
and that there was injustice in the land.
But these things were not new then,
and we are no strangers to them today.
Your people have always failed You in different ways
and in our weakness we are likely to do so again.
Can we then never worship You Lord?

No that cannot be,
for You call us to worship,
You call us knowing our weakness and our spiritual poverty,
and You expect us to respond to Your call.
Was there then a failure of love.
Had worship become a duty
and not a delight?
An outward show for special occasions and no longer a part of everyday life.
Had Your people begun to think that You were only at Jerusalem,
and not interested in what went on elsewhere?

Jesus tell us that worship does not belong to a place;
neither mountain nor Jerusalem.
Worship belongs to You.
We worship with our bodies and our minds,
but our worship must be something of the Spirit,
Your Spirit,

CHAPTER FIVE • *God with Us*

working in us to bring us close to You.
We cannot worship You in words unless the words that we use are true,
for You heard our words, and You know our inmost thoughts,
and these must be the same.
Though we may often deceive ourselves,
we know that we cannot deceive You.
Yet when we come to You in worship
we are burdened with memories of things we have done,
our minds are filled with thoughts about things which are still to do.
thoughts which have their own power to lead us astray,
turning us into paths where You would not have us go.
These thoughts are often not at one with our worship,
and they come between us.

Lord, You call us to worship,
and what You call us to do can never be impossible.
If our worship is to be acceptable,
You must make it so.
So help us today, and every day.
Fill us with Your Holy Spirit
Cleanse us from all things which are a barrier between us,
and enable us to open our hearts and minds to Your presence,
that we might truly worship You
and know Your presence with us.
Not just in this place on Sunday,
but in every place and time.
So that our lives may become truly a part of the life of Your Kingdom,
and we may know ourselves as Your children,
in accordance with Your purpose made known to us in Jesus Christ our Saviour.
Amen.

God Who Calls His People

LORD God, we thank You that in times of old You called Your people to Your service,
that the initiative came from You and not from them.
You brought salvation to them when they were distressed
and freed them from their oppressors,
so that they might become a kingdom of priests,
spreading Your word among the nations.
We thank You that You take that initiative still.
Bidding us to worship You
and calling us to serve You in the world.
A royal priesthood,
a holy nation of Your own people,
called out of darkness into light,
that we might declare Your wonderful deeds to all who will listen.
There is one call, Lord,
one Word addressed to all those whom You would call one people.
But we have not heard it as one people.
We have not shared what we have heard,
neither have we listened through the ears of others.
Open our deaf ears, Lord,
that we might hear more clearly.
Help us to understand how others may hear the words we miss,
and how our understanding may be more helpful to them,
that together we may hear You more clearly.
As did Your people of old,
so may we say with one voice as they did,
'All that the Lord has spoken, we will do'.
Lord, in Your mercy,
Hear our prayer.

CHAPTER FIVE • *God with Us*

AND TO HIM WAS GIVEN DOMINION

LORD God, Creator of Heaven and earth,
You have sent Your Son, Jesus Christ,
to have power and dominion over all the earth,
to be our Master and Lord;
and we bow before Him, acknowledging that authority.
We seek to serve Him
to follow in the way He leads,
showing forth His love in the way we love and serve one another,
but we are not always very good at it,
and sometimes our service is fitful,
and sometimes there has been no service at all,
for love has been absent from our relationships.
We have been arrogant in our service, Lord,
for we have thought ill of those who would serve You differently.
We are ashamed of some of the records of our history.
We have failed to recognise Your authority, Lord,
for You have commanded love, but we have fomented hatred.
And Christian has too often fought against Christian
both in words and deeds.
Lord, help us to accept Your dominion,
in fact as well as in word.
Help us to hear and to obey your instruction of love,
to welcome all those who serve You as our true brothers and sisters,
and to join with them in that service
in all the different forms that service may take.
Help us to share our understanding of Your words
so that we may be able to obey fully that greatest word, that keystone of Your law.
Help us to love one another as You have loved us
and to set aside anything and everything which may divide us in that love.
Lord, in Your mercy,
Hear our prayer.

THE HOPE TO WHICH HE CALLS US

LORD, You remind us so often that this is Your world,
and that in this world nothing happens without Your knowledge.
Before the World began, You were.
You created it all, according to Your plan,
And it has developed as You have foreseen.
The end, too, is part of Your plan,
for You have created it for a purpose.
Your Word has been spoken,
and it will not return to You empty,
but it will achieve the purposes for which it was delivered.
We cannot see the final shape of that purpose, Lord
but we know that there will be a unity of service,
a wholeness, in which Your family will be made one.
When all will dwell together,
made perfect in a perfected world,
that will live in the light of Your glory.
We may only see this vision in faith,
the faith that enlightens the eyes of our hearts,
and fills us with the hope of wonders still to come.
We know that this is a hope for the future, Lord,
but we don't know how long that future may be.
We know that we have a task to carry out,
for until that day of salvation dawns
You have called us to live according to the laws of that Kingdom,
For as Christ lives in us,
so has His Kingdom already come to us.
Lord, help us to live as members of one family,
as people who know they have been redeemed,
and who know, too, that others have been redeemed with them,
to share with them the life of the Kingdom.
So may all who acknowledge Jesus Christ as Lord

be drawn together in one community of sharing love.
Lord in Your mercy,
Hear our prayer.

TOGETHER IN THE FATHERS LOVE

FATHER, You have promised, through Jesus,
to send the Spirit of Truth to those who love You.
Yet those who do truly love You
often see Your truth in different ways,
and we find it difficult to understand why this should be so.
Is it that our minds are clouded by worldly matters,
or overburdened by the weight of tradition and history?
Are we, like James and John, too concerned with our own position,
or that of our own particular church,
and need, like them, to learn Your lesson of humility again?
Lord, cleanse the eyes and the hearts of Your people,
and lift from their shoulders the burdens which bow them down.
Help us to look again upwards,
to see with clearer vision our Lord Jesus Christ,
seated in glory at Your right hand.
In the light of that vision may we be enabled to receive Your Spirit of Truth,
and to comprehend that greater and all-embracing truth
which will bind us together,
overcoming all those imperfect understandings which divide Christian from Christian.
So may we be truly joined,
one with another,
united for ever within the Father's love;
dwelling in that peace which is Christ's promise
to all who love Him.
Lord, in your mercy,
Hear our prayer.

The Peace of God

JESUS said, 'Peace is my parting gift to you,
My own peace, such as the world cannot give'.
But what is this peace;
How do we recognise and know it?
Peace means different things at different times.
To the men on the lake it meant the stilling of the storm,
the quelling of that fierce wind.
To the man of Gerassa it was freedom from torment,
the restoration of his sanity,
freedom to start a new life after the debasement of his illness.
To others it means the end of war and the peril that comes with it.
But others, whom war has not touched, will yet say 'Give me some peace',
and mean no more than freedom from interruption in their work.

But if all these troubles are overcome,
When wars have ended, when storms and troubles cease
will we then know peace?
understand what Jesus meant?
Will our days be full of happiness and content.
Or will yet other troubles rise to break our ease.
I fear it would be so.
For peace is something more than things like these.

True peace lies deep within the soul and mind,
It is a contentment, a trust, a freedom from fear.
But the mind that is just cleared from all disturbing things
and then left empty, is not cured of fear,
and will, if no fears come, invent its own,
to fill that vacant space.
and peace, though once it came, is chased away again.

CHAPTER FIVE • *God with Us*

This is the peace that the world can give,
transient,
temporary,
and of no great lasting value.
But the peace which Jesus offers is such as the world cannot give.
It goes far deeper, and leaves no empty spaces.
For He can fill those empty spaces with His love.
And in that love we know that all is well.
For that love is stronger than anything else around.
The storm may not be stilled,
but it cannot take the place of that great love,
cannot alter the eternal value of our lives.
The world may still bring tribulation,
but that love has overcome the world.
Without that love, there is no lasting peace.
Only when we are filled with that love can we know that peace
which transcends all our troubles.
Jesus said, 'Set your troubled minds at rest and banish your fears'.

I thank Thee, Lord, that here our souls, though amply blest,
Can never find, although they seek, a perfect rest.
Nor ever shall until they lean on Jesu's breast.

Lord, grant us Thy peace.
That peace which passes all understanding.
Help us to put our trust in You
to depend upon You, knowing that You will not fail us.
Fill us with Your love and banish all our fears;
and keep our hearts and minds in the knowledge and the love of Jesus Christ.
For we ask it in His name.
Amen.

A Vision of One World

PULBOROUGH: 27TH OCTOBER 1991

IN THE beginning God created the heavens and the earth.
And the earth was without form, and void.
And the Spirit of God moved over the face of the waters.
We see One World Lord, a formless globe,
spinning its way through the vast spaces of the heavens,
ready to receive the life You give,
formed from the unseen substance of eternity,
setting out on its journey through space and time
to the end You have appointed for it.
An empty world, but full of promise,
a place of endless possibilities,
held together in a unity by the power of Your Spirit,
awaiting the command of Your Word.
And that Word came,
in the thunder of volcanoes,
in the shattering crash of the collision of continents,
in the roar of wind,
the steady drip and flow of water,
the majestic grinding progress of ice,
and in the silence of the division of a cell.
The Word said, 'Let there be life on earth'
and there was life,
in all its wonder and complexity.

And God said, 'Let us make man in our image'
A little lower than the angels
and with dominion over all the works of our hands.
'To multiply and subdue the earth'.
And he did so.

CHAPTER FIVE • *God with Us*

But man rebelled and claimed the earth for his own.
In jealousy and greed he divided God's world
clutching it to himself,
hating the brother whom he should love.
In ignorance he despoiled the world,
using its resources,
and spoiling with pollution that which was not used.
The door was left open for the power of evil to enter,
and he came,
bringing endless trouble in his train,
separating those things which should be kept together,
causing hatred to take the place of love,
and despair the place of hope,
for all who would listen to him.
Mankind has multiplied without thought or care
until the world groans under the weight of his feet
and shudders from the impact of his hand.

The Lord will restore your fortunes and will gather you again to Himself.
The everlasting God, the Creator of the ends of the earth
will not faint or grow weary,
though mankind should continue to his own way
yet he will be recalled.
The way of salvation has been opened
the power of evil has been overcome
though for a time he creates evil still
'In Jesus Christ God was reconciling the world to Himself'.
All the world, not just the favoured few.
In Jesus Christ we may come to understand,
and to see the necessity for Your law of love.
Love for Yourself.
Love for each other.
Loving care for the world which You have made,

and through which You reveal yourself to us.
Loving care for the neighbour,
in whom we see Your presence.
'And there shall be one flock, and one shepherd'.
Who will lead us into green pastures,
and guide us beside the waters of peace
leaving behind the valley of dark shadows.
In His wisdom He will bring understanding and guidance,
that can overcome the storm-clouds of pollution,
and show us how the resources of this world should be used
for the benefit of all.

We look to a future, Lord,
a future in which the wholeness of the world might be restored;
a future in which the world is used with responsibility
and with thought for the effects of actions upon others,
instead of for purely selfish gain.
We look to a future in which the barriers which divide mankind will be overcome.
The barriers of nationality and the memories of past insults that go with them.
The barriers of colour and origins which hide brothers and sisters from each other.
The barriers of class and wealth which make it impossible for us to share Your gifts.
The barrier of spiritual blindness which conceals the true nature of Creation from us.
The barrier of deafness which prevents mankind from hearing Your word of peace.
The barriers of prejudice and religion which dim the radiance of Your glory.
Lord, these are barriers which we have erected
and we have used them to fence around our lives.
They have made it harder for us to know Your presence
and to feel the touch of Your hand.
Because we have set them up
we know that we have to take them down,
but our strength is insufficient.
Help us to open the doors of our lives to Your Holy Spirit,
and in the strength of that Spirit to tear down the barriers

CHAPTER FIVE • *God with Us*

and heal the divisions.
Restore the wholeness of Your World, Father,
Complete the reconciliation which Christ came to bring
That what was one in the beginning may be one again
That mankind may begin to see on earth
something of the unity and the glory
that was Your vision in Creation.
And that we may see ourselves as truly a part of that unity,
members of Your family living in this, Your One World.
Amen.

God's Call

BILLINGSHURST 1ST NOVEMBER 1992

AND Peter said,
'Depart from me, for I am a sinful man, O Lord'.
It was a moment of fear,
a moment when a private world lay open to the light of God,
and it could not stand the disclosure;
it was a moment of realisation
that God was really present in this world as it is.
Present, but un-noticed,
until that sudden, unexpected action opened eyes that had been closed.
It wasn't just the fish,
It was the presence.
It had really been there all along,
it was in the way He spoke, and in the words themselves,
and it was reflected in the crowd as well,
in the way they listened and understood.
But somehow it was an uncomprehended presence.
Until the fish came,
and in their catching gave a new realisation to what was present,
a new authority both to the words and to the man.
It was a holy presence beside which no ordinary man could stand
and remain unashamed.

It was the unexpectedness about it which made it so disturbing
It gave a new understanding of the feelings of Isaiah the prophet
when it happened to him in the Temple.
At one moment it was a perfectly normal day,
filled with its normal business.
One group at the lakeside,
the other in the Temple,

CHAPTER FIVE • *God with Us*

when, without warning,
it was as if a different world had broken through the barriers
which kept it safely outside the world we know.
An awesome different world,
One which brought us into the very presence of God,
a presence which suddenly confronted us
in all its strangeness and awesome power
right in the middle of the world we thought we knew and understood.
And nothing can ever be quite the same again.

God seldom comes when He is expected.
And His call to us can be surprising.
We may see Him in the sudden beauty of the sunset
or read His Word in the rainbow's arch,
or hear Him speak in the silence of a hallowed building.
There may be a new vision in the words of others
as they speak of Him.
But, however He may come to us,
He always calls us to look at Him again
to see Him with fresh eyes
and to recognise His authority and His power.
But with that recognition there is something else to see,
a task to do,
a need to meet,
a word or deed of love to carry.
And there is a question in His eyes.
'Choose whom you will serve, and choose today!
Will it be me, or those other gods,
The gods of a busy world that you claim for yourself?'
But seldom is there any need of words,
the presence, and the vision of purpose which it brings
is enough to demand a response,
a decision, yes or no

CHAPTER FIVE • *God with Us*

a decision in which we know there is only one right answer,
however much we may fear to give it.

Lord, we know that we are unworthy of Your love,
and that we are indifferent servants of Your kingdom.
And nowhere do we know that so well as when we feel Your presence,
and see Your glory around us.
We are people of unclean lips, members of a sinful company
and we fear the judgement which that presence brings before us.
And yet, even as we fear,
we know our deep need of You
and of the cleansing which You alone can bring to us.
Our hearts are restless until they find their rest in You
and we cannot ask that You remain far from us.
For we know there is no life away from Your presence.
And so, we pray that You will come to us,
Show us Your Glory,
and speak to us of the Salvation You have wrought for us
in Jesus.
That in Your presence we may see clearly those things which You call us to do.
And in the power of Your Holy Spirit We may draw upon Your strength
Strength that we will need,
to undertake those tasks.
So come to us, Lord.
Banish our fears,
and equip us for the work of Your Kingdom.
That we may follow our Lord and Master, Jesus Christ
in the service which He offered to men and women in Your name.
For it is in His name we ask it.
Amen

I am Alpha and Omega

BILLINGSHURST 3RD JANUARY 1993

'BEHOLD, I am the Alpha and the Omega,
The first and the last,
The beginning and the end', says the Lord our God.
And we may marvel at the words.
For we stand in the midst of time
looking back over countless ages
to an act of creation we can barely envisage.
Creation of a universe that is so big, so diverse,
that our minds cannot take it in.
A universe that is expanding, growing, changing,
in ways that few can begin to understand.
Yet we can look back and see the print of Your hand
in those early beginnings,
and catch a hint of Your purpose
in the pattern of that unfolding,
even while our understanding of the pattern changes
as we continue to study it.
And so we may know that You are truly the beginning Lord,
even though we cannot see clearly what the beginning is.

We do not only look to the past, Lord,
We turn and look to the future,
seeking to understand the end as we seek to comprehend the beginning.
But our eyes cannot see into the future,
neither can our instruments comprehend it.
Yet we know that there must be an end,
for the processes that keep the universe alive are finite.
The fuel that runs the sun and stars will one day be consumed,
and they, like us, will die.

But is that the end?
We think not.
For in the unfolding of life we sense a purpose,
Your purpose Lord,
something which gives meaning to this universe You have made.
And it is a purpose in which we have a place,
and a part to play.
And if You have a purpose in creation,
You will be there at the end,
to see that purpose fulfilled,
for that purpose is a part of Your being.
And so we can know You, Lord,
as the Omega,
the end of all things,
the last as You are also the first.

But what of us today,
People who are not at the beginning,
and who do not know how far away the end might be,
knowing only that our life is short,
and eternity long.
Where do we find You, Lord?
Some have feared that You designed Your universe,
and sent it out upon the sea of time,
like a comet spinning in endless space,
far from its parent sun,
until the fullness of time,
the workings of Your laws bring it again
out of the dark and trackless wastes of space
into its father's light.
Returning for judgement after long years of loneliness.
But You, Lord, are never far from Your creation
And you have shown Your presence to us

CHAPTER FIVE • *God with Us*

To Your prophet of old You declared Your presence,
Using Your name, the eternal 'I am'.
Making it plain that You were still present in Your world,
although it was a presence only seen in dreams and visions,
for no one had ever seen Your face,
and only the eye of faith could truly know You.
Time and eternity could still be far apart
and Paradise no more than a gleam of light
on a far distant horizon.

The Word, that eternal Word,
that when uttered gave form and purpose to creation itself,
was made flesh and dwelt among us,
full of grace and truth.
Born not into the social remoteness of worldly power
where only a few might know,
and still less understand.
The Word became a part of our life
at the lowest and humblest level.
Born as a child in a borrowed shelter,
far from the comforts of home,
welcomed by our representatives,
rich and poor,
wise and humble,
yet rejected by many.
In Him we have seen Your presence in our lives;
You have shown us both beginning and end;
drawn from eternity into the limits of created time.
In Him we have the assurance
that our short lives lie within the boundaries of Your love,
and are part of Your eternal being;
and that death,
the deadly terminator of the created lives of time,

can hold no power over us
for he has been banished from Your realm by the power of that same love.
In the life of Your Son, the incarnation of Your eternal Word,
We have seen for ourselves and know
that You are not only Alpha and Omega,
beginning and end,
You are always present in Your creation,
In all times and all places.

Lord God,
help us to live our lives in the knowledge of Your eternal presence.
Fill us with the confidence of faith.
Grant to us that sureness of vision by which we may know
that our birth,
our life,
and our death,
are all within Your purpose and Your care.
That just as You are the Alpha and the Omega of creation,
so You are to each one of us whom You have created.
Help us to know, and to take ourselves, that great truth,
that all of our lives here on earth
are part of the everlasting life of Your Kingdom.
And in that assurance, Lord,
help us to live lives that are in accordance with Your purposes for us;
lives that will fit us for the light and joy of Your Heavenly realm.
For we ask it in the name above all names,
Jesus Christ, Your eternal word of truth and love.
Amen.